COOK IT QUICK

THE COMPLETE SEAFOOD COOKBOOK
THE STEAK BOOK

Arthur Hawkins

COOK IT QUICK

203 DELICIOUS HALF-HOUR RECIPES

AVENEL BOOKS
NEW YORK

decorations by Linda Huber

517R00319
© MCMLXXI by Arthur Hawkins

This edition published by Avenel Books
a division of Crown Publishers, Inc.
by arrangement with Prentice-Hall, Inc.

f g h

Library of Congress Catalog Card Number: 72-138479

Manufactured in the United States of America

for
Gil
Art
Dick
Julian

CONTENTS

A place for everything, and everything in its place must be the rule, in order that time may not be wasted in looking for things when they are wanted, and that the whole business of cooking may move with the regularity and precision of the well-adjusted machine.

Isabella Beeton
248 Strand, London
England
1861

COOK IT QUICK

INTRODUCTION

You've been working all day, and now you've got to fix dinner. Everybody's hungry. There isn't much time. What's your next move? Easy. You just open a package of frozen vegetables, get out the hamburger or chops, and you're in.

But wait, that's what you fixed for dinner yesterday—and the day before. Monotonous, isn't it?

According to statistics, 5/7 of the average cook's cooking days are concerned with just this sort of throw-it-together-and-get-it-over-with meal. Probably, 5/7 of your dinners take less than half an hour to prepare—or you wish they did. And your weekly dinner menu looks something like this:

Monday: hamburger
Tuesday: lamb chops
Wednesday: pork chops
Thursday: hamburger
Friday: spaghetti
Saturday (guests for dinner):   grand casserole de la maison with truffles, cèpes, wild rice, tossed salad with Roquefort dressing, hot garlic bread, petits fours, and demitasse
Sunday: leftovers, if any

If the above-described shoe fits, don't wear it. Throw it away and start all over again—from scratch. You don't have to serve the same old stuff every day. Plan ahead—enlarge your culinary repertoire. If you could have up your sleeve a selection of 15 (only 15) different dishes, you could run through an entire month of dinners repeating only a few of your top favorites—and that's living!

Your menu for the month could look something like this:

steak au poivre
eggs Benedict
cheese fondue, Neuchâteloise
chopped steak, Roquefort
scaloppine alla Milanese
Maryland crab cakes
pan-broiled chops
Schnitzel à la Holstein

spaghetti and meatballs
chef's salad
pan-broiled chicken breasts
half-hour beef stew
broiled halibut steak
chicken livers with mushrooms
fettucini all' Alfredo

13

All these dishes can be prepared well within half an hour. You don't like some of the dishes listed? No problem. Make up your own selection—there are more than 200 recipes in the pages that follow from which to choose.

Quick and easy recipes are only one way to make cooking a pleasant task. Another is to make sure you have an orderly and efficient kitchen to work in. As Mrs. Beeton, who wrote her cookbook 100 years before this one, said, "A place for ever/thing and everything in its place . . . ."

Take a new look at your kitchen. Examine your tools and utensils with a critical eye. Throw out, or store away, those that have been accumulating for years, yet are hardly ever used. Shift those used for holiday or weekend cooking to a less accessible closet or cabinet. Locate or relocate the remaining basic equipment so that you can lay your hands on what you want when you want it. Hang things on the wall—on peg boards—near the stove (if that's where you use them most often), or near the sink. You'll be surprised how much easier cooking is—and how much faster—when everything is at your fingertips, and when you don't have to root through a lot of clutter to find what you need.

Now take inventory. Check the utensils you have on hand against what you ought to have. The following list will help. It includes just about everything that will make efficient cooking a pleasant experience.

blender (not indispensable
   but very, very handy—a
   time-saver, too)
bowls (various sizes)
carving board
colander
deep-fat fryer with thermostat
   (if you like deep-fried foods)
double boiler
knives (various types)
measuring cup
measuring spoons

meat grinder (for leftovers)
pans (various types)
potato peeler
pots (various sizes)
pressure cooker (not always
   recommended, but a help
   at times)
rotary beater
spatula
utensil rack (with fork, cake
   turner, slotted spoon, spoon)
wire whisk

But an orderly, well-tooled kitchen isn't the whole story. What good is a pot to cook in when there's nothing on hand to cook? Nothing can be more discouraging to a tired or busy cook than an empty salt box—or one you can't find. Oh! there it is behind those old things on the top shelf! Yes, supplies have a way of accumulating—especially those that don't spoil. Before you know it, shelves become cluttered with half-empty packages of stuff you don't really need anyhow. You can save time—and patience, too—if you tuck away all those seldom-used supplies on top shelves. Arrange things so that the foods and accessories you use most often are most conveniently located, and then stock up with the essentials you are missing. Keep a check list of staples, herbs and spices, and canned and frozen goods so that you can replenish items as they are used up. The following checklist should get you started

STAPLES

flour (all-purpose)
instant potatoes
jams and jellies
mustard (dry and prepared)
olive oil
pasta (spaghetti, noodles,
    vermicelli, macaroni, etc.)
rice (the quick kind)
sugar
syrup (maple or corn)
Tabasco sauce
tomato paste
vegetable oil
vinegar
Worcestershire sauce

PERISHABLES
(REFRIGERATED)

butter and/or margarine
celery
cheeses
eggs
lettuce
milk
parsley
tomatoes

PERISHABLES

garlic
onions
potatoes
shallots

CANNED GOODS

baked beans
mushrooms
soups
spaghetti, macaroni, etc.
tomato sauce
tomatoes
tuna fish, salmon

HERBS AND SPICES

basil
bay leaf
cayenne
chives
curry powder
marjoram
nutmeg
orégano
pepper (whole and ground)
rosemary
sage
thyme

15

Now add a few basic fresh or frozen foods . . .

chicken livers	fruit juices
chicken parts	ground beef
chops	shellfish (scallops, shrimp, etc.)
cutlets	steaks
desserts	vegetables
fish fillets	

All set? Now you're equipped to sail through any of the 200-odd recipes in this book. Cook it quick . . . but eat it slow. Enjoy!

1
EGG
DISHES

Ostriches, turkeys, geese, peacocks (correction: peahens), ducks, chickens, pigeons, guinea-hens, pheasants, quail, plovers, and gulls all lay eggs. So do the other birds—and the fish—and the reptiles. Almost all eggs can be used for food. But there are limitations. Ostrich eggs are slightly unavailable—so are plover eggs. Gull eggs have a fishy flavor; duck and goose eggs are oily. So, when we talk of eggs in the kitchen, it's the eggs of the female chicken we mean.

As a first-class food, hen's eggs are hard to beat. They're nutritious, plentiful, convenient to buy, easy to store and, if treated with respect, remain fresh for a long time. Fresh eggs are heavy (they feel well-filled when shaken), but as they get older they become lighter as evaporation takes place through the porous shell.

Best of all, though, you can cook eggs almost any way you want and eat them at any meal. Simply prepared—scrambled, fried, poached, or soft cooked—they make an excellent breakfast dish. Shirred, poached, or made into omelets with other foods added, eggs make an ever-variable and satisfying luncheon or dinner dish. It is with these more elaborate recipes that *Cook It Quick* is concerned.

The omelet is the basis for so many great egg dishes that it will pay you well to take time to learn how to make it expertly. Good omeletiers have good frying pans made of heavy cast aluminum with sloping sides about 2 inches deep and measuring about 8 inches across. The pans are never used for cooking anything but omelets, and they are never washed. In general, there are three types of omelets: the French omelet, the puffy omelet, and the flat omelet. And here's how you make them:

18

FRENCH OMELET *time: 6 minutes / servings: 1*

3 eggs	break the eggs into a bowl, add the salt and water, and
½ teaspoon salt	beat with a wire whisk (or fork) just enough to blend
1 teaspoon cold water	the whites and yolks
1 tablespoon butter	get the omelet pan good and hot, drop in the butter and
white pepper	swish it around, pour in the omelet mixture, shake the pan back and forth scrambling the eggs quickly and briefly with the flat side of a fork

let the omelet set, lifting it with the fork to allow the uncooked part to run under (if you're going to add mushrooms, onions, tomatoes, or other garnishes, do it at this point)

fold in half and roll onto a heated platter. season with pepper, dot with additional butter, and serve at once

the omelet should be creamy and soft on the inside (what the French call *baveuse*), golden on the outside. if it comes out dry, throw it away and start over again. one other thing, an omelet made with more than 3 eggs is not easy to cook uniformly. if you wish to serve several people, make separate omelets for each

19

Don't serve lapwing eggs to strangers. Cooking them is against the law and you might get yourself in trouble.

PUFFY OMELET *time: 8 minutes / servings: 1*

3 eggs, with yolk and white separated	beat the yolks in a bowl until thick using a wire whisk (or fork) add the hot water, salt, and a pinch pepper
3 tablespoons hot water	
½ teaspoon salt	beat the whites until stiff and fold them into the yolks until the mixture is well blended
white pepper	
1 tablespoon butter	get an omelet pan moderately hot, drop in the butter and swish it around
	spoon the egg mixture into the pan and spread it evenly. cook slowly and evenly
	when the omelet is well-puffed and delicately golden underneath, slide the pan under the broiler and quickly brown the top
	fold, roll onto a heated platter, season with a little pepper, dot with additional butter, and serve at once

BACON OMELET *time: 10 minutes / servings: 1*

20

4 slices bacon cut into ½-inch pieces	fry the bacon lightly and add to the eggs while beating them
	proceed as in making a 3-egg French or flat omelet

FLAT OMELET *time: 8 minutes / servings: 1*

to make a flat omelet, follow the recipe for French omelet but do not scramble the eggs. the result is a sort of thick egg pancake

the basic omelet—French, puffy, or flat—is the starting point for innumerable variations. *Larousse Gastronomique,* the French encyclopedia of cooking, lists more than 100, and there are variations of these variations. following are recipes for a selection of omelets I believe to be the most popular, most unusual, or most exciting. the recipes are given for one omelet. if you're making more than one, and are using a filling, prepare a proportionally larger amount for additional omelets, but cook the omelets separately

21

OMELETTE AUX
FINES HERBES *time: 14 minutes / servings: 1*

here's another great French omelet. I believe it would be difficult to find a menu in all of France that does not list *omelette aux fines herbes,* but the herbs used vary a great deal according to the whim of the chef or the availability of the herbs

1 tablespoon finely chopped fresh parsley

1 teaspoon finely chopped fresh (or frozen) chives

1 teaspoon finely chopped fresh tarragon

1 teaspoon finely chopped fresh shallots or spring onions

1 teaspoon finely chopped chervil

pinch thyme

(any, or all, of the above herbs will make a good omelet—you can even add a touch of garlic)

mix the *fines herbs* together thoroughly and put them into the hot butter before adding the beaten eggs

proceed as in making a 3-egg French omelet

22

OMELETTE
BONNE FEMME *time: 21 minutes / servings: 1*

here is a really great omelet—very popular in France where they spell it *omelette*. very filling, too. serve it as a one-dish meal

3 slices bacon, cut into ½-inch pieces	put the bacon bits, butter, onions, potato cubes, salt, and pepper into a small skillet, cover and cook for 15 minutes
1 tablespoon butter	
½ onion, chopped	spoon this filling onto a 3-egg French omelet before folding
1 medium potato, cooked and cubed	fold, turn onto a heated platter and serve garnished with chopped parsley
½ teaspoon salt	
dash pepper	
chopped parsley	

OMELETTE
CHASSEUR *time: 14 minutes / servings: 1*

2 tablespoons finely chopped chicken livers	sauté the chicken livers and mushrooms in the butter for 5 minutes
2 tablespoons finely chopped mushrooms (fresh or canned)	season. spoon this filling onto a 3-egg French omelet before folding, reserving a little for garnishing
1 tablespoon butter	
½ teaspoon salt	
dash pepper	fold, turn onto a heated platter, and serve with a little of the filling spooned on top

23

CHEESE OMELET *time: 12 minutes / servings: 1*

4 tablespoons grated Gruyère, chopped American, or almost any other kind of cheese	add the cheese to the eggs while beating them proceed as in making a 3-egg French or flat omelet

CHICKEN LIVER OMELET *time: 20 minutes / servings: 1*

2 chicken livers, coarsely chopped	sauté the chicken livers in the butter for 5 minutes
1 teaspoon butter 2 tablespoons brandy	add the brandy, flame for a minute, and then remove the livers from the pan
1 teaspoon butter ¼ teaspoon tomato paste ½ teaspoon flour	stir the butter, tomato paste, flour, chicken stock, and wine into the pan. cook for 5 minutes. then add the flambéed chicken livers
¼ cup chicken stock ⅛ cup red wine ½ teaspoon salt	season, and using a slotted spoon, lightly spread this filling onto a 3-egg French omelet before folding
dash pepper	fold, turn onto a heated platter, spoon the remaining sauce over the top of the omelet, and serve

24

CROÛTON OMELET   *time: 12 minutes / servings: 1*

¼ *cup croûtons (packaged, or your own bread cubes fried in butter until crisp)*	add the croûtons and parsley to the eggs while beating them
1 *teaspoon minced parsley*	proceed as in making a 3-egg flat omelet or puffy omelet

OMELETTE À LA PROVENÇALE   *time: 12 minutes / servings: 1*

1 *tablespoon olive oil*	cook the garlic in the oil for 2 minutes, remove and discard
½ *clove garlic (optional)*	
½ *cup peeled, seeded, diced, and drained tomatoes (or use canned tomatoes if you have to)*	add the tomatoes, season with salt and pepper, and cook for 2 minutes
½ *teaspoon salt*	add the tomatoes and the parsley to a 3-egg French omelet before folding
dash pepper	
1 *teaspoon minced parsley*	fold, roll onto a heated platter, dust with paprika and serve
dash paprika	

Candles on the table add to the enjoyment of the meal.

25

HAM OMELET   *time: 10 minutes / servings: 1*

3 tablespoons finely chopped cooked ham	add the ham to the eggs while beating them
(Smithfield-type ham, if you can find it, is something special)	proceed as in making a 3-egg flat omelet. or sauté the ham in a tablespoon of butter and spoon it onto a French omelet before folding
	fold and serve

HUNGARIAN OMELET   *time: 14 minutes / servings: 1*

4 tablespoons diced lean ham	sauté the ham, onions, and paprika in the butter for 5 minutes. season with salt
4 tablespoons finely chopped onions	
½ teaspoon paprika	add this mixture to the eggs while beating them and proceed as in making a 3-egg flat omelet
1 tablespoon butter	
½ teaspoon salt	

26

The king of Spain was taking a walk in the country. He became hungry and dropped into a peasant's house and asked for some food, quick. The peasant beat up a few eggs, cooked them in oil, and served them to the king in a trice. "Quel homme leste (what a quick man)!" exclaimed the king. And the word omelet was born? Wrong. The word omelet, in Spanish, is *tortilla!*

OMELETTE À LA JARDINIÈRE *time: 12 to 16 minutes / servings: 1*

4 tablespoons chopped mixed cooked vegetables (carrots, turnips, string beans, peas, potatoes, etc.)	sauté the chopped vegetables in butter 5 minutes and season with salt and pepper
1 tablespoon butter	add this mixture to the eggs while beating them and proceed as in making a 3-egg flat omelet
½ teaspoon salt	
dash pepper	serve garnished with hot asparagus tips
3 or 4 cooked asparagus tips	

MUSHROOM OMELET *time: 10 to 12 minutes / servings: 1*

3 tablespoons thinly sliced fresh or canned mushrooms	sauté the mushrooms in butter for 4 minutes (if canned, 2 minutes will do it). season with salt and pepper
1 tablespoon butter	add the mushrooms to the eggs while beating them, reserving a few slices for garnishing
½ teaspoon salt	
dash pepper	
	proceed as in making a 3-egg flat or French omelet
	serve dotted with butter and garnished with the sliced mushrooms

27

LEFTOVERS OMELET *time: 12 to 18 minutes / servings: 1*

4 tablespoons chopped cooked leftovers (chicken, beef, flaked fish, kidney, lamb, pork, sausage, vegetables—anything)	sauté the leftovers in the butter for 5 minutes
1 tablespoon butter	add this mixture and the cream to a 3-egg French omelet before folding
2 tablespoons heavy cream (sweet or sour)	fold and serve garnished with chopped parsley
chopped parsley	

OMELETTE PARMENTIER *time: 12 to 18 minutes / servings: 1*

this is one of my favorite omelets, but I've never tasted a good one anywhere but in France. French chickens seem to have a special talent for producing special eggs—or could it be what French cooks do to them?

4 tablespoons finely diced potatoes, raw or cooked	sauté the potatoes, parsley, and salt in butter for 3 minutes (longer, if potatoes are raw). do not brown
1 teaspoon chopped parsley	
½ teaspoon salt	spoon this mixture onto a 3-egg French or puffy omelet before folding
1 tablespoon butter	
	fold, turn out onto a heated platter and serve garnished with a little of the parsley

28

ONION OMELET *time: 12 minutes / servings: 1*

3 tablespoons chopped onion	sauté the onion and paprika gently in the butter for 3 minutes. do not brown. season with salt
½ teaspoon paprika	
1 tablespoon butter	
½ teaspoon salt	spoon the onion onto a 3-egg French omelet before folding
chopped parsley	fold, place on a heated platter and serve garnished with chopped parsley

OMELETTE À LA PAYSANNE *time: 12 to 16 minutes / servings: 1*

4 slices bacon cut into ½-inch pieces	fry the bacon until crisp and remove from the pan. add the potatoes to the bacon fat and sauté for 3 minutes (longer if raw). do not brown. season with salt
3 tablespoons thinly sliced potatoes, raw or cooked	
½ teaspoon salt	mix the bacon and potatoes and add half to a 3-egg French omelet before folding
	fold. serve with the remaining bacon-potato mixture on top

29

SEAFOOD OMELET   *time: 11 to 15 minutes / servings: 1*

4 tablespoons chopped cooked lobster, shrimp, scallops, or any other seafood or mixture of seafoods

1 teaspoon chopped parsley

1 tablespoon butter

½ teaspoon salt

dash paprika

cook the seafood and parsley in the butter for 2 minutes. season with salt

add the mixture to a 3-egg French omelet before folding

fold, roll onto a heated platter, dust with paprika and serve

SPANISH OMELET   *time: 19 minutes / servings: 1*

½ clove garlic

1 tablespoon butter

1 tablespoon oil

1 tablespoon finely chopped onion

1 tablespoon finely chopped green pepper (or pimento)

½ cup peeled, seeded, diced, and drained tomatoes

1 tablespoon chopped parsley

1 teaspoon chopped watercress

cook the garlic in the oil and butter for 2 minutes, remove and discard

add the onion, pepper, tomatoes, and parsley and sauté gently for 4 minutes

add this mixture to a 3-egg French omelet before folding

fold and serve garnished with chopped watercress

if you wish to make a variety of omelets for a lot of people, whisk up a bowl-full of eggs and have on hand a ladle or cup that measures out just the right amount for each omelet

make up several kinds of filling: chopped herbs, parsley, grated cheese, chopped ham, etc. . . . have plenty of butter on hand in tablespoon measures. now you're ready for quick cooking, gourmet style

as you cook the omelets, remove them to heated plates and stick them into a 200° oven, and, unless you keep them there too long, they will stay hot without cooking or drying out

---

POACHED EGGS

poaching an egg requires no great knowledge—just a little care. you start with a one-quart saucepan full of boiling water, add 1½ teaspoons salt and 1 teaspoon of vinegar. break the egg into a saucer so that you can be sure the yolk is intact and slide it into that part of the water that is boiling most rapidly

turn the heat down so that water just simmers and let the egg remain 3 minutes or until the yolk is firm when pressed with the back of a fork. remove carefully with a skimmer or slotted spoon, drain, and serve according to your favorite recipe

poached eggs may be kept warm without cooking in warm salted water until ready to serve. note: it is best not to attempt poaching more than 4 eggs at a time

31

POACHED EGGS
BENEDICT *time: 7 minutes plus 5 / servings: 2*

eggs Benedict would not ordinarily be included among dishes quickly made because Hollandaise sauce—a prime requisite of the dish—is tedious, time-consuming, and sometimes tricky to make. however, there is a very successful blender-Hollandaise that can be accomplished quickly and easily. if you're a blender-owner, turn to the index for the recipe and you're in

4 thin slices ham	sauté the ham slices in butter for 5 minutes
2 tablespoons butter	
4 eggs	meanwhile poach the eggs and toast the muffins
2 English muffins, split	put the ham onto the English muffin halves, spoon a
1 cup hot Hollandaise sauce (see index)	poached egg onto each, cover with Hollandaise sauce, and serve at once

POACHED EGGS
AU GRATIN *time: 10 minutes / servings: 2*

4 eggs	poach the eggs and place them into a buttered shirring pan or into 2 individual ramekins
6 tablespoons grated Parmesan cheese	
1 cup béchamel sauce (see index)	sprinkle with Parmesan cheese, cover with béchamel sauce, and top with more cheese
	bake in a preheated 350° oven until top is brown (about 4 minutes)

32

POACHED EGGS ON TOMATOES, ITALIAN STYLE *time: 14 minutes / servings: 2*

4 thick slices tomato	sauté the tomato slices in olive oil for 5 minutes. cook a clove of garlic with the tomato, if you like
4 tablespoons olive oil	
1 clove garlic (optional)	
1 teaspoon salt	remove the tomato slices to a heated platter, season with salt, pepper, and orégano. cover each with a poached egg and serve
dash pepper	
pinch orégano	
4 poached eggs	

SHIRRED EGGS

this is what the French call *Oeufs sur le plat,* the *plat* being a small individual pan or oven-proof ramekin in which the eggs are oven-cooked. you always lubricate the shirring dish with a little melted butter before breaking the eggs into it, and you often cook them with garnishes and/or top them with sauces. shirring takes about 5 minutes

SHIRRED EGGS WITH CHICKEN LIVERS *time: 10 minutes / servings: 1*

33

put cooked, sliced chicken livers into a shirring pan with 1 tablespoon butter, heat for 3 minutes, then break in 2 eggs. season with salt and pepper and cook in a preheated 350° oven until eggs are set

SHIRRED EGGS WITH
HAM AND CHEESE *time: 10 minutes / servings: 1*

put a little chopped or sliced cooked ham into a buttered shirring dish. heat for a few minutes, drop in 2 eggs, season with salt and pepper, and sprinkle with shredded cheese. slide dish into the oven until eggs are brown

SHIRRED EGGS
WITH MUSHROOMS *time: 10 minutes / servings: 1*

sauté some sliced or chopped mushrooms in a buttered shirring dish for 5 minutes, add 2 eggs, season with salt and pepper, and cook in a preheated 350° oven until eggs are set

SHIRRED EGGS *time: 10 to 15 minutes plus 5*
WITH VEGETABLES *servings: 1*

put cooked vegetables (asparagus tips, peas, spinach, carrots, or pearl onions) into a shirring pan with a little butter. cook for 5 or 10 minutes, then add 2 eggs. season with salt and pepper, cover with béchamel sauce if you wish (see index), and cook in a preheated 350° oven about 5 minutes

34

SHIRRED EGGS WITH CROÛTONS
time: 10 minutes / servings: 1

1 tablespoon butter	melt the butter in a shirring dish, add the croûtons, and cook for 2 minutes
3 tablespoons croûtons	
2 eggs	drop in the eggs, season with salt and pepper, add the cream, and top with additional croûtons
salt	
pepper	
2 tablespoons cream	bake in a preheated 350° oven about 8 minutes or until eggs are set

SHIRRED EGGS, GRAND-DUC
time: 10 minutes plus 15 servings: 1

1 tablespoon butter	melt the butter in a shirring dish, drop in the eggs, season with salt, cover with Mornay sauce, sprinkle with grated cheese, and dot with butter
2 eggs	
½ teaspoon salt	
½ cup Mornay sauce (see index)	bake in a preheated 350° oven until eggs are set and golden-crusted (about 8 minutes)
1 tablespoon grated cheese	
4 asparagus tips	serve garnished with hot asparagus tips

35

SHIRRED EGGS
FLORENTINE *time: 12 minutes / servings: 1*

1 tablespoon butter	melt the butter in a shirring dish, add the spinach, and
1 tablespoon chopped cooked spinach (fresh or frozen)	season with salt. drop in the eggs, sprinkle with cheese, and add the heavy cream
½ teaspoon salt	
2 eggs	bake in a preheated 350° oven about 8 minutes or until eggs are set
2 tablespoons grated Parmesan cheese	
2 tablespoons heavy cream	

for an extra rich Florentine, use ½ cup Mornay sauce (see index) instead of cream. add 15 minutes to the preparation time

SHIRRED EGGS,
À LA LORRAINE *time: 10 minutes / servings: 1*

1 tablespoon butter	line a buttered shirring dish with bacon and cheese
2 slices cooked bacon	slices. break in the eggs, season with salt, pour a ring
2 thin slices Gruyère cheese	of cream around the yolks, and bake in preheated 350°
2 eggs	oven about 8 minutes
½ teaspoon salt	
thick cream	

36

SHIRRED EGGS
WITH LEFTOVERS   *time: 10 minutes / servings: 1*

put 2 generous tablespoons cooked leftovers (chopped chicken, flaked fish, hash, etc.) into a buttered shirring dish. cook for a few minutes, then add 2 eggs. season with salt and pepper and cook in a preheated 350° oven until eggs are set

---

FANCY
SCRAMBLED EGGS   *time: 5 to 8 minutes / servings: 2*

the plain, everyday, breakfast scrambled egg assumes a new gastronomic taste when blended with crab meat, mushrooms, ham, cheese, or other good things. first break 3 eggs into a bowl and beat with a whisk or fork until well blended but not frothy. add 1 tablespoon heavy cream and 2 or 3 tablespoons cooked crab meat, chopped mushrooms (sautéed in butter), cooked cubed ham, or cubed cheese. season with salt. pour this mixture into a well-buttered skillet and cook over low heat, stirring constantly, until firm and creamy but not dry (remember, they will continue to cook a little after you have dished them out of the skillet). tarragon, chives, and parsley, when cooked with scrambled eggs, complement their flavor

CREAMED EGGS time: 22 minutes / servings: 4

here is a versatile and popular dish. you can season the sauce with any number of condiments—curry powder, paprika, chili powder, tomato paste, etc.—and you can serve the creamed eggs on a base of cooked rice, buttered toast, English muffins, or waffles

8 eggs	cook the unshelled eggs in boiling water for 18 minutes. remove the shells, and cut the eggs into slices or quarters
2 cups béchamel sauce *(see index)*	
salt	
pepper	while the eggs are cooking, make the béchamel sauce
6 slices buttered toast	mix the sauce with the eggs, season with salt and pepper, and serve on buttered toast, garnished with paprika and parsley
paprika	
minced parsley	

CURRIED EGGS time: 22 minutes / servings: 4

season béchamel sauce (see index) with curry powder to your taste, proceed as in making creamed eggs, and serve on cooked rice

38

EGGS RANCH STYLE *time: 22 minutes / servings: 4*

called in Mexico *huevos rancheros*, these eggs are served on *tortillas*, thin cakes made of masa flour. in Texas and Southern California, where ranch style eggs also abound, the *tortillas* are often omitted

3 tablespoons chopped onion	cook the onion and garlic in the butter until golden then add the pepper, tomato, seasonings, and chicken broth
1 clove garlic, minced	
2 tablespoons butter	
2 tablespoons chopped green pepper	cook over low heat until vegetables are soft and the sauce has thickened
1 large tomato, peeled, seeded, squeezed dry, and chopped	fry or scramble the eggs and serve with the sauce poured over them
few drops Tabasco sauce	
¼ teaspoon orégano	
1 teaspoon salt	
½ teaspoon pepper	
½ cup chicken broth	
8 eggs	

39

PIPÉRADE *time: 16 minutes / servings: 4*

this is a hearty Basque dish, very popular with the local country people—and very filling

2 medium onions, chopped	in a heavy frying pan sauté the onions, tomatoes, and pimentos in bacon fat until soft and golden (about 5 minutes)
2 medium tomatoes, peeled, seeded, squeezed dry, and chopped (or use canned tomatoes, if you have to)	
4 canned pimentos, chopped	gradually pour in the beaten eggs, scrambling vigorously until firm but not dried out. season with salt, pepper, and a little marjoram
bacon fat	
6 eggs, beaten	
salt	
pepper	
marjoram	

SCOTCH WOODCOCK *time: 10 minutes / servings: 2*

this is the dish—as the story goes—that the Scotch wife serves her husband when he returns empty-handed from a day of bird hunting. it's rich and filling, but woodcock it's not

2 English muffins, split	toast the English muffins and spread with butter and anchovy paste. arrange on 2 heated plates
anchovy paste	
4 eggs	
4 tablespoons cream	mix the eggs, cream, salt, and pepper. beat slightly
salt	scramble the eggs over low heat and serve on the toasted muffins, garnished with paprika
pepper	
paprika	

2
CHEESE
DISHES

Eating cheese is a most pleasant way of taking your vitamins. And, along with each bite, you get an extra dividend of protein and calcium. Hard or soft, mild, sharp, or pungent, cheeses are most often taken straight with a piece of bread, a cracker, or to enhance the flavor of other foods. But there are cheese dishes appetizing and satisfying enough to substitute for main meat courses. Those that fit into a quick cook's time schedule are given here. Remember only that cheese must be cooked at a low temperature and for a short time so it doesn't end up tough or stringy.

WELSH RABBIT #1 *time: 12 minutes / servings: 4*

even if you spell it "rarebit," you still pronounce it like the bunny and you make no mistake about it. make no mistake about the cheese you use either. the better the cheese, the better the rabbit—or rarebit

1 pound cheese cut into small bits (Cheddar or Cheshire type—either mild or sharp)	put the cheese, butter, and seasonings into a saucepan (or double boiler) and cook very slowly over low heat, stirring occasionally, until cheese is melted
2 tablespoons butter	
1 teaspoon dry mustard	
1 teaspoon paprika	slowly add the ale (or beer), stirring constantly
1 teaspoon Worcestershire sauce	add the egg, continuing to stir until thickened
salt	pour over toast and serve at once
pepper	
½ cup ale (or beer)	
1 egg, slightly beaten	
toast	

The quickest and most popular dessert is ice cream. Dress it up by adding a spoon of *Grand Marnier* or other liqueur, or by dusting with grated coconut or powdered malted milk.

WELSH RABBIT #2 *time: 12 minutes / servings: 4*

1 pound cheese cut into small bits (Cheddar or Cheshire type—either mild or sharp) *1 cup cream*	put the cheese, cream, and seasonings into a saucepan (or a double boiler), and cook very slowly over low heat, stirring occasionally, until cheese is melted
1 teaspoon dry mustard *1 teaspoon Worcestershire sauce*	add the egg, stirring constantly until thickened pour over toast and serve at once
few grains cayenne *salt* *1 egg, slightly beaten* *toast*	

to make a big deal of welsh rabbit, spoon it over slices of chicken breast on buttered toast, top with rashers of bacon, and place under the broiler until the bacon is crisp. or spoon the rabbit over heated broccoli, asparagus, or sliced tomatoes, fortified with sliced ham. or add it to poached eggs, sliced hard-cooked eggs, lobster, or shrimp. there are many ways of making a great meal with welsh rabbit as a base

TOMATO RABBIT   *time: 14 minutes / servings: 4*

2 tablespoons butter	melt the butter in a saucepan over low heat, gradually add the flour and then the milk, stirring constantly
2 tablespoons flour	
½ cup milk	
1 cup grated sharp cheese	when thickened, add the cheese, sugar, and salt. stir until cheese is melted and ingredients are well blended
1 teaspoon sugar	
1 teaspoon salt	
½ cup canned tomato purée	stir in the tomato purée and serve on hot buttered toast, garnished with bacon
6 slices buttered toast, cut diagonally in half	
4 slices cooked bacon	

Donkey meat is considered by many to be superior in flavor to that of horse.

45

CHILALY *time: 8 minutes / servings: 2*

1 tablespoon chopped green pepper	sauté the pepper and onion in butter for 2 minutes
1 tablespoon chopped onion	add the tomatoes and cook 4 minutes longer
1 tablespoon butter	
¼ cup canned tomatoes, drained	reduce the heat and add the cheese and seasonings. cook very slowly until cheese melts
½ pound soft, mild cheese, cut into small pieces (cream, mozzarella, Muenster, etc.)	stir in the milk and egg
salt	when the mixture thickens, spoon it over toast and serve
cayenne pepper	
1 tablespoon milk	
1 egg, slightly beaten	
4 slices toast	

46

CHEESE FONDUE #1 *time: 16 minutes / servings: 4*

this is a sort of Swiss rabbit—with a kick. you serve it in a fondue pot (or chafing dish) with a spirit flame beneath. you and your guests surround the fondue and dunk with hunks of French bread impaled on long two-tined forks. A bottle of cool white wine goes well as an accompaniment

1 clove garlic, cut	rub the inside of a fondue pot or chafing dish with cut garlic
2 cups dry white wine	
4 cups grated Gruyère or Swiss cheese (or a mixture of the two)	pour in the wine, heat, and gradually stir in the cheese until completely melted
2 teaspoons cornstarch	
¼ cup Kirsch	mix the cornstarch and Kirsch and stir into the cheese mixture. season with nutmeg and salt
¼ teaspoon nutmeg	
pinch salt	serve hot with hunks of French bread for dunking
French bread	

To save time and trouble, keep a package of frozen chopped onions in the freezer compartment.

47

CHEESE FONDUE #2 *time: 16 minutes / servings: 4*

here's a milder fondue leaving out the garlic, wine, and Kirsch. you might find it somewhat lacking in character, but its mild flavor has a way of attracting friends

½ pound grated Gruyère or Swiss cheese (or mixture of both) *8 egg yolks*	mix the cheese, egg yolks, nutmeg, salt, and pepper in a fondue pot or chafing dish over low heat stirring constantly
¼ teaspoon nutmeg *pinch salt*	add the butter, bit by bit, stirring constantly
½ teaspoon pepper *¼ pound butter* *½ cup cream* *French bread*	when the mixture thickens add the cream, stir, and serve with hunks of French bread

FONDUE
NEUCHÂTELOISE   *time: 16 minutes / servings: 4*

1 clove cut garlic	rub the inside of an earthenware (or enamel) casserole with garlic, pour in the wine, and bring to a slow simmer over low heat
2 cups dry white wine (Riesling, Chablis, etc.)	
½ pound Swiss cheese or Gruyère (or a mixture of the two), finely cut	dredge the cheese with flour, stir it into the hot wine, and season to taste
flour	
salt	stir in the Kirschwasser, remove from the stove and place over a spirit flame to keep hot
pepper	
nutmeg	spear hunks of bread with a fork and dunk!
4 ounces Kirschwasser or other dry fruit brandy	
crusty French bread broken into bite-size bits	

49

CHEESE CASSEROLE   *time: 30 minutes / servings: 4*

butter	butter the toast, cut into narrow strips, and line the bottom and sides of a buttered baking dish
4 slices lightly toasted bread	
½ pound mild cheese, cut into pieces (mozzarella, Cheddar, Muenster, provolone)	mix the remaining ingredients, pour into the dish, and bake in a preheated 375° oven for 20 minutes
2 eggs, slightly beaten	
1 cup cream	
½ teaspoon dry mustard	
½ teaspoon paprika	
½ teaspoon salt	
cayenne pepper	

CHEESE "SOUP" *time: 15 minutes / servings: 4*

don't get any wrong ideas about this dish. cheese it is, but soup it certainly is not. try it and see

1 loaf crusty French bread	cut the bread into large slices, place in a large saucepan, sprinkle with salt, and cover with bouillon
salt	
1 can bouillon	
4 tablespoons butter	when the bouillon has been soaked up by the bread, add the butter in bits and mash with a potato masher. cook, stirring all the time
½ pound grated Gruyère cheese	
2 medium onions, chopped	gradually add the cheese and heat gently for 10 minutes
1 tablespoon butter	

meanwhile, using a separate pan, brown the chopped onions in butter

serve the "soup" in bowls topped with the sautèed onions

51

3
PASTA
DISHES

All the forms of pasta are made from wheat, kneaded into a stiff dough and extruded through perforated cylinders.

They come out as spaghetti, vermicelli, tagliatelli, fettucini, linguine, macaroni, etc., depending upon thickness and shape. Noodles are a form of pasta containing eggs. Almost all varieties are available ready-made and prepackaged. And they are all quick and easy to prepare. You simply follow the directions on the package. Or be guided by the following recipe: Boil 4 quarts of salted water in a large pot (this should take about 12 minutes). Drop in the spaghetti or other pasta (do not break into pieces) and cook until tender but firm—about 8 minutes. If you're in doubt about the doneness, chew on a piece to test. Drain in a colander (or warm napkin—as the Romans do). Stir in the sauce and serve.

Sauces, too, are available prepackaged—in cans or glass-packed. Select your favorite type—meat, meatless, marinara, or white clam—heat, and stir into the freshly cooked spaghetti. You will find that there is a difference in thickness, oiliness, aroma, and flavor among the available brands, so choose the brand you like best. (You can always doctor it up with garlic, orégano, or tomato paste to suit your taste.)

There are also good quick homemade sauces you can make in less than half an hour if you plan your time well. The trick is to start the sauce first, dropping the pasta into boiling water 8 to 10 minutes before the sauce is finished. Everything will then be ready at the same time.

Here's a count-down procedure that works . . .

SPAGHETTI WITH
OIL AND GARLIC *time: 25 minutes / servings: 4 to 6*

INGREDIENTS	TIME	STEP	PROCEDURE
4 quarts water	−25 min	(1)	put the water on to boil
1 pound package spaghetti	−10 min	(2)	drop the spaghetti into the boiling
½ cup olive oil			water
2 cloves garlic	−6 min	(3)	in a small saucepan heat the oil to the smoking point and turn off the heat. chop the garlic and add it to the oil. let stand
6 or 8 sprigs parsley			
grated Parmesan cheese			
	−3 min	(4)	mince the parsley and add it to the oil
	−2 min	(5)	drain the spaghetti and stir in the oil and garlic
	0 min	(6)	serve with or without Parmesan cheese, as desired

To dress up a simple dinner quick . . . garnish with celery, a couple of olives, a slice of tomato or hard-cooked egg, pickled beets, a dab of mint jelly or cranberries, potato chips, canned cold asparagus, etc. . . .

SPAGHETTI ALLA
NAPOLITANA *time: 25 minutes / servings: 4 to 6*

this is a tricky dish to do in half an hour, but it can be done if you stick to the following time table . . .

INGREDIENTS	TIME	STEP	PROCEDURE
4 quarts water	−25 min	(1)	put the water on to boil
¼ cup olive oil	−17 min	(2)	heat the oil in a skillet. chop the onion and garlic, drop into the oil, and sauté gently
2 cloves garlic			
1 onion			
3 tablespoons chopped ham	−14 min	(3)	chop the ham and sausage and add to the skillet
½ pound Italian sausage			
1 cup canned tomato sauce	−10 min	(4)	add the tomato sauce and bouillon to the skillet. drop the spaghetti into the boiling water
½ cup canned bouillon			
1 pound package spaghetti	−2 min	(5)	drain the spaghetti and stir in the sauce
grated Parmesan cheese	0 min	(6)	serve, topped with grated cheese

56

SPAGHETTI WITH
TOMATO SAUCE   *time: 25 minutes / servings: 4 to 6*

INGREDIENTS	TIME	STEP	PROCEDURE
4 quarts water	−25 min	(1)	put the water on to boil
½ cup olive oil			
	−12 min	(2)	chop the garlic and sauté it gently in the oil
2 cloves garlic			
pinch orégano			
	−10 min	(3)	add the seasonings, tomato paste, and bouillon to the oil, cover and simmer. drop the spaghetti into the boiling water
pinch basil			
pinch thyme			
2 cans tomato paste			
1 cup canned bouillon	−2 min	(4)	drain the spaghetti and stir in the sauce
1 pound package spaghetti	0 min	(5)	serve with grated Parmesan cheese
grated Parmesan cheese			

SPAGHETTI AND
MEATBALLS   *time: 25 minutes / servings: 6*

follow the recipe for Spaghetti with Tomato Sauce, but double the amount of oil and garlic. form ¼ pound chopped beef into tiny balls and sauté in the oil with the garlic for 5 minutes. remove from the oil and add to the spaghetti just before serving

57

FETTUCINI ALL'
ALFREDO *time: 20 minutes / servings: 4 to 6*

if you are an American visitor in Rome, the first thing you are likely to do is pay a visit to Alfredo's for a dish of his fettucini for which he was awarded—so the story goes—an 18-carat gold fettucini fork. but one of your problems might be to decide which of two Alfredos is the real and original Alfredo. don't let it worry you. both restaurants do a fine fettucini and both will go through the ritual of presenting you with a "gold" fork. what many people don't realize is that this is actually a simple dish, and one you can easily and quickly prepare at home

1 pound package slim egg noodles	boil the noodles in a large pot of salted water until tender but still firm (about 8 minutes should do it), drain and dry in a hot napkin
salt	
¼ pound soft sweet butter	
¼ cup heavy cream	place the noodles on a heated platter or bowl, add the butter, cream, and half the cheese, and toss until well mixed using two forks
1 cup grated Parmesan cheese	
freshly ground pepper	serve topped with pepper and the remaining Parmesan cheese

FETTUCINI ALLA
ROMANA *time: 20 minutes / servings: 4 to 6*

mash 8 anchovy fillets to a paste and mix them well into the butter and cream. proceed as in making Fettucini all' Alfredo

NOODLES
WITH PESTO *time: 20 minutes / servings: 4 to 6*

1 pound package thin egg noodles

salt

4 cloves garlic, minced

½ cup dried basil (or a handful fresh leaves with stems removed)

½ cup fresh parsley with stems removed

2 tablespoons pine nuts

½ cup grated Parmesan cheese

¼ cup olive oil

2 tablespoons soft butter

boil the noodles in a large pot of salted water until tender but firm (about 8 minutes)

meanwhile, prepare the pesto: put the garlic, basil, parsley, pine nuts, ¼ cup Parmesan cheese, and olive oil into the container of a blender and mix to the consistency of mayonnaise

drain the noodles, dry in a hot napkin, and put into a heated bowl. add the pesto and butter and toss until well blended. serve with Parmesan cheese

TAGLIATELLI
WITH HAM *time: 20 minutes / servings: 4 to 6*

1 pound package slim egg noodles	boil the noodles in a large pot of salted water until tender, but firm (about 8 minutes). drain and dry in a hot napkin and place into a warm bowl
salt	
¾ cup warm chopped ham (or prosciutto)	
¼ pound sweet butter, melted	mix the ham and butter and add to the noodles, with the cheese, tossing together until well blended
¼ cup grated Parmesan cheese	

LINGUINE WITH
CLAM SAUCE *time: 20 minutes / servings: 4*

this dish, if prepared in the home, can be complicated and time-consuming, but you can do a creditable job using canned clam sauce

cook 1 pound of linguine according to the directions on the package and place in four deep dishes that have been preheated

heat a can of white clam sauce and pour over the linguine. the thin, garlicky sauce settles to the bottom leaving the clam pieces on top of the pasta—the trick is to keep mixing as you eat

4
SEAFOOD
DISHES

Seafood is the ideal food for quick cooking. Deep-fat or pan fried, poached or broiled, fish never requires longer than half an hour to fix—unless, of course, you have in mind doing a *haute cuisine* dish with forcemeat stuffing and an elaborate sauce, or a casserole. Neither does shellfish—it's quick, too.

If you find yourself on the Eastern Shore of Maryland, in the vicinity of Charleston, South Carolina, or anywhere along the Florida coast, in New Orleans or San Francisco, or on the coast of New England, the seafood you cook could be same-day fresh. I have it on firsthand authority from a spot called Mitchell's Corner (made famous by Herman Melville?) that the natives of Nantucket Island pamper their palates on a year-round basis with the delicacies from the waters surrounding them.

If you can't find the time to visit the fish market and buy your seafood right off the ice, there is a liberal selection of frozen fish and shellfish in most supermarkets which you can buy and stow away in the freezer compartment—ocean perch, haddock, and flounder fillets, for example; halibut, swordfish, and salmon steaks; shrimp, scallops, lobster tails, crab meat, and oysters; and many seasonal delicacies such as smelt, sea squab (blowfish), and brook trout. Then there are, of course, good canned seafoods you can keep on hand almost forever—tuna, salmon, crab meat, sardines, and kippers, to name a few.

How do you cook seafood? You fry it. Yes, according to statistics, Americans—by a four to one margin—prefer their fish and shellfish fried! So, if you are one of the great majority, better rush right out and acquire a fast-acting, easy-to-use deep-fat fryer with an automatic thermostat for fool-proof timing. Or buy yourself a deep-fat frying basket and a thermometer, if you do not already have them. But meanwhile don't neglect the delicate and succulent poached dishes—or the robust ones you can make in the broiler.

DEEP-FRIED
OYSTERS *time: 20 minutes / servings: 2*

1 egg	beat the egg until foamy and stir in the milk and seasonings
3 tablespoons milk	
salt	dip the oysters into the egg, then into cracker dust
pepper	place the breaded oysters, a few at a time, into a wire
1 dozen large oysters, shucked	basket and immerse into 365° deep-fat for 2 to 4 minutes or until golden (add 1 or 2
cracker dust (or dry bread crumbs)	minutes to the cooking time if the oysters are frozen)
cooking oil	serve garnished with chopped parsley and tartar sauce
tartar sauce (bottled, or see index)	
chopped parsley	

DEEP-FRIED
SOFT CLAMS *time: 20 minutes / servings: 2*

1 egg	beat the egg until foamy and stir in the milk and seasonings
½ cup milk	
salt	dip the clams into the egg-milk mixture and then into the bread crumbs
pepper	
2 dozen shelled soft clams	place the breaded clams, a handful at a time, into a wire
dry bread crumbs	basket and cook in 350° deep-fat for 2 to 3 minutes or
cooking oil	until golden
tartar sauce (bottled, or see index)	serve with tartar sauce

63

DEEP-FRIED
FISH FILLETS *time: 20 minutes / servings: 2*

1 pound fish fillets (flounder, sea perch, sole, etc.) *salt*	pat the fillets dry with a paper towel, sprinkle with salt and pepper and dredge with flour
pepper *flour* *1 egg*	dip the fillets into egg that has been beaten with a little water and then into the bread crumbs
1 tablespoon water *dry bread crumbs* *cooking oil*	place the breaded fillets one at a time into a wire basket and fry in 365° deep-fat for 3 to 5 minutes (4 to 6 minutes if frozen)
tartar sauce or sauce rémoulade (bottled, or see index)	serve with tartar sauce or sauce rémoulade

DEEP-FRIED
FISH STICKS *time: 20 minutes / servings: 2*

use ¾ pound fish sticks for 2 servings and follow directions for cooking fish fillets, but heat the cooking oil to 375° instead of 365°

DEEP-FRIED SCALLOPS OR SHRIMP *time: 20 minutes / servings: 2*

½ cup flour

½ teaspoon baking powder

salt

1 egg

½ cup milk

1 pound scallops (bay or sea)
or
1 pound shelled raw shrimp

cooking oil

tartar sauce (bottled, or see index)

1 lemon, cut into wedges

mix the flour, baking powder, and salt. beat the egg and milk until fluffy. combine the two to form a batter

wipe the scallops or shrimp dry with a paper towel and dip into the batter

place the scallops, a few at a time, into a wire basket and immerse into 365° deep-fat and cook until golden (bay scallops: 2 to 3 minutes, sea scallops, slightly longer. shrimp: 3 to 5 minutes, depending upon size. if frozen, add 1 or 2 minutes to the cooking time)

serve with tartar sauce and lemon wedges

Oysters *won't* spoil if you boil them in oil.

65

DEEP-FRIED
SMELT OR
SEA SQUAB   *time: 20 minutes / servings: 2*

1 egg	beat the egg and stir in the milk and seasonings
½ cup milk	
salt	dip the smelt or sea squab into the egg mixture, then into the bread crumbs
pepper	
1 dozen smelt, cleaned but with heads intact or ½ dozen sea squab	place the breaded fish, a few at a time, into a wire basket and immerse into 365° deep-fat for 2 to 4 minutes or until golden (cook 1 or 2 minutes longer if frozen)
bread crumbs	
cooking oil	serve with tartar sauce and lemon wedges
tartar sauce (bottled, or see index)	
1 lemon, cut into wedges	

SOFT SHELL CRABS *time: 10 to 21 minutes / servings: 2*

use 4 small, or 6 tiny, crabs for 2 servings. crabs should (correction: must) be alive when purchased. have your fish man clean them for you or do it yourself. (all you have to do is cut off the face, then raise the top shell at its points and scrape away the spongy stuff beneath)

to deep fry, follow the procedure for cooking scallops or shrimp, adding 1 minute to the cooking time if the crabs are large

or you might take the quick, easy, and delicious way by pan-broiling the little crabs in butter. (dust them lightly with flour and cook them on each side for about 5 minutes, or until golden)

serve either way on buttered toast with a lemon wedge on the side—and a little tartar sauce, if you like

PAN-FRIED SEAFOOD

to pan-fry or sauté, prepare the seafood as in deep-frying and cook in a heavy skillet containing ¼-inch of cooking oil heated almost to the smoking point. seafood must be cooked in a single layer and should be turned for uniform browning on both sides

67

Alligator is not readily available in the American market. Even if it were, its musky flesh—taken mostly from the flappers or paws —could not easily be cooked in half an hour. So there's really no place for it in this book. Besides, it actually doesn't taste very good. Forget it.

MARYLAND
CRAB CAKES   *time: 16 minutes / servings: 2*

1 tablespoon chopped onion

1 tablespoon butter

½ pound fresh, cooked crab meat

1 egg, beaten

¼ teaspoon dry mustard

¼ teaspoon salt

dash pepper

dash cayenne

2 tablespoons mayonnaise

bread crumbs

cooking oil

sauté the onion in the butter for 1 minute

combine all the ingredients except the bread crumbs and form into 4 cakes

roll in bread crumbs, and place into a heavy frying pan containing ⅛-inch fat, hot but not smoking, and fry on each side about 5 minutes or until golden

---

In any kitchen where there is consistently a dearth of leftovers, the cook must be doing *something* right.

PAN-BROILED
SEAFOOD

to pan-broil seafood, pat it dry with a paper towel, flour lightly, and cook in a heavy skillet which is oiled just enough to prevent sticking. the trick is to get the heat just right so that the seafood will brown properly and at the same time cook through

pan-broiling is quick—fillets, fish sticks, scallops, shrimp, and small fish require less than 15 minutes to cook

even large fish (halibut, salmon and swordfish steaks, bluefish, striped bass and flounder, etc.) can be cooked easily in about 20 minutes

GRILLED FISH

whole small fish (smelt, sea squab, brook trout, etc.) and split larger fish (bluefish, mackerel, sea bass, pompano, etc.) cook very well, and quickly, under the broiler. pat the fish dry with a paper towel, brush with oil, season with salt and pepper, sprinkle lightly with flour, and place on an oiled broiler rack (split fish should be placed skin-side down). slide under a preheated 500° broiler about 3 inches from the heat and cook until fish flakes when fork-tested (15 to 20 minutes, depending upon thickness). unless fish is very thick, it will not need to be turned

BOILED LOBSTER   *time: 20 minutes / servings: 2*

2 medium lobsters (about 2 pounds each), live *3 quarts boiling water* *2 tablespoons salt* *butter*	put the live lobsters* into a large pot of boiling salted water and simmer for 10 minutes split along the stomach from head to tail, and serve hot with melted butter. or cool and serve with mayonnaise or tartar sauce

if you can spare a little extra time add a carrot, a bay leaf, a clove, a few peppercorns, a stalk of celery, a little vinegar, and 1 onion, sliced, to the boiling water

---

* if you're squeamish about dumping the live lobsters into the boiling water, put them into the water before turning on the heat. experiments at Cornell University indicate that this method lulls them to sleep gradually so that they depart from this world in a drowsy state of euphoria

GRILLED LOBSTER *time: 30 minutes / servings: 2*

2 medium lobsters, live

cooking oil

butter

pierce the lobsters in the backs between the body and the tail with a sharp knife. this severs the spinal cord and, so help me, it doesn't even hurt them

put the lobsters on their backs and slice open from head to tail with a sharp knife. do not cut through the back shells

spread open and remove the black line and the stomach. crack the claws

place in the broiler shell-side down, brush with oil, and broil about 20 minutes, or until browned. serve with melted butter

71

POACHED FISH
FILLETS

poaching is the method of cooking fish best suited for fillets such as flounder, sole, ocean perch, and haddock, but it also works well with any small non-oily fish. poaching, of all cooking methods, probably does the best job of preserving the true flavor of fish. besides, it's easy—and quick

you start with a poaching liquid—milk, cream, salted water, white wine, fish stock, chicken broth, a combination of several liquids, or a prepared *court-bouillon* (which we will pass by in this book because of the time required to make it)

then you proceed as follows:

1. using a skillet, heat about an inch of poaching liquid to just below boiling
2. add the fillets one at a time, and simmer gently until they flake when tested with a fork (4 to 6 minutes)
3. remove them to a heated platter, taking great care not to break, and serve with butter, a lemon slice, and minced parsley—or with your favorite sauce— béchamel, egg, curry, herb, mushroom, Mornay, newburg, or wine sauce (see index)

OYSTER OR
CLAM STEW *time: 6 minutes / servings: 2*

the Oyster Bar in Grand Central Station, New York, has been serving me oyster stews since 1925, and I know that others have been enjoying them long before I made the discovery. indeed, there seems no reason to doubt that more oyster stews have come out of Grand Central than trains. the recipe for putting together this most famous of all oyster stews is no mystery since the action takes place before your very eyes. you can duplicate the Grand Central stew in your own home—and quickly—by carefully observing the following rules:

2 tablespoons butter	put the butter, Worcestershire, paprika, pepper, and celery salt into a saucepan and cook for 1 minute
1 teaspoon Worcestershire sauce	
½ teaspoon paprika	add the oysters or clams and let them froth for a minute, then pour in the liquor and boil hard for 1 minute longer
½ teaspoon pepper	
½ teaspoon celery salt	
1 dozen medium oysters or cherrystone clams	reduce the heat, pour in the milk or cream, and cook slowly, stirring constantly to prevent curdling. do not allow to boil
1 cup oyster liquor mixed with clam juice	
1 pint milk, half-and-half, or cream	pour into bowls, add a pat of butter to each, and garnish with paprika

73

PAN-BROILED
SHAD ROE *time: 8 minutes / servings: 2*

*1 large (or 2 small) pair
fresh shad roe*

boiling water

1 tablespoon salt

1 tablespoon vinegar

2 tablespoons butter

6 toast points, buttered

2 slices cooked bacon

place the shad roe into a skillet, cover with boiling water, add the salt and vinegar, and simmer 2 minutes

drain off the water, add the butter, and pan-broil until golden brown on all sides

serve on buttered toast points, with a rasher of bacon on each serving

SALMON LOAF *time: 30 minutes / servings: 2*

1 cup canned salmon

½ cup chopped onion

¼ cup fine soft bread crumbs

½ tablespoon chopped parsley

salt

pepper

dash Worcestershire sauce

2 cups béchamel sauce (see index)

mix all the ingredients and form into a loaf. put into a buttered baking dish and bake in a preheated 375° oven until golden (about 20 minutes)

serve with hot béchamel sauce which you can make while the loaf is baking

---

TUNA FISH CAKES *time: 13 minutes / servings: 2*

1 can tuna fish

1 egg, beaten

2 tablespoons mayonnaise

2 slices bread, soaked in milk and squeezed almost dry

¼ teaspoon dry mustard

dash cayenne pepper

bread crumbs

cooking oil

combine the tuna, egg, mayonnaise, bread, and seasonings. form into 4 cakes and roll in bread crumbs

fry in a heavy skillet containing a little oil until golden on both sides (about 6 minutes)

75

CREAMED TUNA
OR SALMON *time: 15 minutes / servings: 2*

1 can tuna fish or salmon

2 hard-cooked eggs, shelled and chopped

2 cups béchamel sauce (see index)

butter

4 slices toast

combine the canned fish and eggs with the sauce, heat, and serve on buttered toast (or rice)

76

5
CHICKEN
DISHES

A quick dish, chicken isn't!

Fowl, under ordinary circumstances, will never make it from barnyard (or even marketplace) to the dinner table in half an hour. But three factors have induced me to include a few chicken dishes in this book. First, there's the presence in the market of easy-to-handle chicken parts, greatly decreasing preparation time. Second, there is the presence in many of today's kitchens of quick deep-fat frying and pressure-cooker equipment. And third, chicken just happens to be one of the great leftovers that inhabit the American refrigerator—especially on Monday.

So here is a scant dozen recipes for fixing chicken in half an hour or less.

Wine makes even the simplest meal seem festive. Serve any type you enjoy with any meal but, in general, remember that dry white wines (chilled) go best with seafood and chicken.

DEEP-FRIED
CHICKEN *time: 30 minutes (?) / servings: 4*

2½ pounds young chicken parts	dry the chicken parts with a napkin and season with salt and pepper
salt	
pepper	prepare the batter according to directions on the package
prepared batter	dip the chicken parts into the batter and fry until golden brown (about 15 minutes) in deep fat at 350° (be strict about the temperature and fry only a few pieces of chicken at a time). drain on paper
cooking fat	

instead of batter, you can dip the chicken parts in lightly beaten egg, then in bread crumbs

PAN-BROILED
CHICKEN BREASTS *time: 30 minutes (?) / servings: 4*

2 pounds boneless chicken breasts, cut in half	flatten the chicken breasts by pounding with a skillet or the side of a cleaver
salt	
pepper	season with salt and pepper, cook in a heavy, oiled skillet until tender and brown (about 20 minutes). remove to a heated serving platter
2 tablespoons oil	
¼ cup dry white wine	stir the wine into the skillet juices and pour over the breasts

79

you can garnish chicken breasts with all sorts of good things: broiled mushrooms, broiled tomatoes, bacon, asparagus tips, etc. . . .

SAUTÉED CHICKEN
BREASTS *time: 30 minutes (?) / servings: 4*

2 pounds boneless chicken breasts, cut in half	flatten the chicken breasts by pounding with a skillet or the side of a cleaver, season with salt and pepper, and dredge with flour
salt	
pepper	in a heavy skillet, mix the butter and oil and heat almost to the smoking point. sauté the breasts until golden (about 5 minutes), turning often
flour	
½ cup butter	
½ cup cooking oil	
	cover and cook slowly about 20 minutes or until tender

QUICK CHICKEN
FRICASSEE *time: 30 minutes / servings: 4*

2½ pounds young chicken parts	season the chicken parts with salt and pepper, dredge with flour, and brown quickly in butter and oil in a pressure cooker (about 10 minutes)
salt	
pepper	add 1 cup hot water, cover, bring to 15 pounds pressure, and cook 10 minutes
flour	
3 tablespoons butter	
3 tablespoons cooking oil	reduce the pressure, stir in the cream, and serve on cooked rice
1 cup hot water	
½ cup heavy cream	
2 cups cooked rice	

80

CREAMED CHICKEN
AND MUSHROOMS *time: 16 minutes / servings: 4*

2 tablespoons butter

2 tablespoons flour

1 cup canned chicken broth

*1 cup cubed leftover chicken
(or canned chicken)*

*½ cup sliced canned
mushrooms*

salt

pepper

pinch nutmeg

1 egg, slightly beaten

1 tablespoon cream

1 tablespoon sherry

paprika

6 slices toast

melt the butter, stir in the flour, and then the broth. add the chicken and mushrooms, and simmer 8 minutes

add the seasonings, egg, cream, and sherry, heat and stir constantly for 2 minutes

decorate with paprika and serve on toast points

almost as good if you don't have mushrooms

81

If, after eating a mushroom, you find yourself experiencing an indefinable malaise accompanied by stomach cramps, abundant salivation and vomiting, followed by delirium, fainting, and prostration, you can be pretty sure that the mushroom was a toadstool

QUICK CHICKEN
À LA KING *time: 20 minutes / servings: 2*

*1 cup cubed leftover chicken
(or canned chicken)*

*½ cup sliced canned
mushrooms*

*¼ cup chopped canned
pimentos*

*1 cup béchamel sauce (see
index)*

1 egg yolk

1 tablespoon sherry

3 slices buttered toast

mix all the ingredients, heat
in a saucepan or double
boiler, and serve on toast

CHICKEN OR
TURKEY HASH *time: 10 minutes / servings: 2*

to 2 cups chopped leftover cooked chicken or turkey, add 1 cup
leftover gravy and chopped parsley. season to taste with salt,
pepper, and Tabasco. serve with rice

QUICK CHICKEN CROQUETTES   *time: 20 minutes / servings: 2*

2 cups ground cooked chicken

2 tablespoons cream

mix the ground chicken, cream, and egg and form into 4 croquettes

1 egg, slightly beaten

dry bread crumbs

dip the croquettes into bread crumbs and fry in a butter-oil mixture until golden

3 tablespoons butter

3 tablespoons oil

serve topped with mushroom sauce and sprinkle with parsley

1 cup mushroom sauce (see index), or 1 can cream of mushroom soup

chopped parsley

CHICKEN LIVERS EN BROCHETTE   *time: 10 minutes / servings: 2*

1 pound chicken livers, cut in half

thread the livers and bacon alternately onto skewers

3 slices bacon, cut into quarters

melted butter

grill about 3 inches from the heat in the broiler, turning and brushing frequently with melted butter

CHICKEN LIVERS
WITH BACON *time: 15 minutes / servings: 4*

8 slices bacon	broil the bacon until crisp in a heavy skillet, remove, and keep warm
1½ pounds chicken livers, cut in half	
salt	season the chicken livers with salt and pepper, dredge lightly with flour, and sauté about 10 minutes in the hot bacon fat. do not overcook
pepper	
flour	
4 slices buttered toast	serve on toast garnished with bacon slices

try stirring a couple of tablespoons Madeira wine (or dry sherry) into the skillet juices and pour the sauce over the chicken livers

---

CHICKEN LIVERS
WITH MUSHROOMS *time: 12 minutes / servings: 4*

2 slices bacon, chopped	in a heavy saucepan, sauté the bacon, shallot, and butter for 4 minutes
1 shallot, chopped (or ½ tablespoon chopped onion)	
2 tablespoons butter	flour the chicken livers slightly, add them to the skillet, and cook 4 minutes longer
1½ pounds chicken livers, cut in half	
flour	add the mushrooms and cook 2 minutes longer
½ cup canned mushrooms	serve garnished with chopped parsley
chopped parsley	

84

6
MEAT DISHES

Meat is not only the favorite food on everybody's everyday menu,
it is also the prevalent offering of all quick cooks the world
over. Steaks, chops, cutlets, ground meat, and sausages can all
be served up in a matter of minutes and require no special talent
or treatment to make them palatable. In this book I try to include
all the more routine dishes—those encountered regularly—and
then add a good measure of unexpected ones, just as easy to do
—all with cooking time of half an hour or less.

PAN-BROILED STEAK *time: 10 to 14 minutes / servings: 4*

2½ pounds steak, 1 to 1½ inches thick (porterhouse, sirloin, club, rib, or Delmonico)

salt

ground pepper

1 tablespoon butter

trim off excess fat and slash fatty edges of steak in several places to prevent curling. pat dry with towel to promote even browning

get a heavy skillet good and hot and toss in the steak, do not pre-salt. do not cover the skillet. do not add water or fat

pour off any excess fat that might accumulate (or the steak will fry)

when the steak is nicely browned, turn, season the cooked side with salt and pepper, and continue broiling until blood appears on cooked surface

remove from the heat immediately and you will have a perfect medium-rare steak. if you prefer it medium, cook it a little longer

OVEN-BROILED
STEAK *time: 25 to 30 minutes / servings: 6*

2½ pounds steak, 1½ to 2 inches thick (sirloin or porterhouse)

salt

freshly ground pepper

(steak for oven-broiling must be at least 1½ inches thick or it will become done on the inside before it is brown on the outside.) trim off excess fat and slash fatty edges to prevent curling. pat steak dry with towel to promote even browning

turn the broiler to top temperature, place the steak on a greased broiler rack and slide into the broiler as close to the heat as possible

how long do you broil steak? who knows? how big is your broiler? do you have natural, artificial, mixed, or bottled gas? or do you have an electric broiler? how do you like your steak—rare, medium, or well-done (ugh)? to be sure of getting the doneness you want, slit the steak near the bone and note the color of the meat inside. a steak weighing more than 2½ pounds or thicker than 2 inches is out of the quick cook's class and will almost surely take more than half an hour

88

If you happen to be boiling some potatoes or eggs, add a few extra ones and you'll have the makings for a quick salad the next day.

STEAK AU POIVRE *time: 30 minutes / servings: 4*

2½ pounds steak, 1½ inches thick (porterhouse, sirloin, club, or Delmonico)

3 tablespoons whole peppercorns

salt

¼ cup olive oil

¼ cup cognac

½ pint heavy cream

minced parsley

coarsely crush the peppercorns (put them in a towel and sock it to them with the bottom of a skillet —or use a mortar and pestle)

trim the excess fat from the steak, season on both sides, and pound the peppercorns into both sides until meat is thickly coated

heat the olive oil to the very smoking point in a heavy skillet and broil the steak to desired doneness on both sides

remove the steak to a heated platter

discard all but a tablespoon of the drippings. add the cognac. heat and flame for about 1 minute, add the cream, stir, and heat. when the sauce thickens, pour it over the steak and garnish with minced parsley

sometimes this wonderful dish is made without the cream. the option is yours. I have also known people to scrape away excess peppercorns before serving. I like the pepper

STEAK LOIRE *time: 20 minutes / servings: 4*

4 ½-pound boneless steaks, 1-inch thick (club, Delmonico, filet mignon, or even minute steaks)

4 tablespoons butter

½ pound mushrooms, sliced

1 cup chopped chives

1 teaspoon salt

½ teaspoon pepper

½ teaspoon butter

2 tablespoons dry sherry

2 tablespoons cognac

3 tablespoons cream blended with 1 teaspoon flour, 1 tablespoon dry mustard, and 1 teaspoon lemon juice

broil the steaks about 2 minutes on each side in 2 tablespoons of the butter, using a heavy skillet. remove to a heated platter

using the same skillet, gently sauté the mushrooms and chives in the remaining 2 tablespoons butter for about 5 minutes

season with salt and pepper, add the sherry, and cook 1 minute longer

warm the cognac, ignite it, and pour into the sauce

stir in the cream-flour-mustard-lemon mixture, simmer for a few minutes, and pour over the steaks

STEAK DIANE   *time: 20 minutes / servings: 4*

4 ½-pound boneless steaks, 1-inch thick (club, Delmonico, or filet mignon)	trim away excess fat, if any, and tie up loose ends
¼ pound butter	place steaks between two sheets of waxed paper and pound until about ½-inch thick
4 tablespoons chopped shallots (or spring onions)	
2 tablespoons Worcestershire sauce	brown the steaks quickly on both sides in a large heavy skillet and remove to a hot platter
1½ tablespoons dry mustard	using the same skillet, simmer the butter, shallots, and seasonings until brown
1 teaspoon salt	
½ teaspoon freshly ground pepper	return the steaks to the skillet and cook in the sauce about 2 minutes on each side
4 tablespoons cognac	
minced parsley	warm the cognac, ignite, and pour over the steaks. serve garnished with parsley

you can do this dish beautifully—and sensationally—in a chafing dish right at the table. quick, too—but you'd better try it out privately before you attempt to show off in front of guests . . . just in case . . .

91

FILETS MIGNON
FLAMBÉS *time: 25 minutes / servings: 4*

4 ½-pound slices of filet mignon	rub all the edges of the steaks with cut garlic
1 clove garlic, cut	shake a little salt into a heavy skillet and place over high heat. pan-broil the steaks until crisp and brown on the outside and rare on the inside
4 slices French bread sautéed in 2 tablespoons butter	
2 tablespoons cognac	place the sautéed bread slices on a heated platter and cover with the steak slices
salt	
freshly ground pepper	
minced parsley	warm the cognac, ignite, and stir into the skillet
	pour the pan juices over the steaks, season with salt and pepper and garnish with parsley

---

Serve goat's beard just like you do asparagus or salsify.

92

FLANK STEAK AU
BEURRE NOIR *time: 15 minutes / servings: 4*

a well-seasoned flank steak from a choice steer is a great piece of meat—boneless, easy to handle, flavorful. but it's thin and apt to become overdone, so cook it quick over high heat, and serve it hot

2 to 2¼ pounds flank steak	rub the steak on both sides with cut side of garlic,
1 clove garlic, cut	brush with oil, and broil quickly on both sides in a
1 tablespoon oil	heavy hot skillet
salt	remove steak to a warm platter or serving board.
pepper	season with salt and pepper
2 tablespoons butter	cut diagonally into thin slices
	brown the butter in the pan juices and pour over the steak and serve

PORTERHOUSE
STEAK WITH
MUSHROOMS *time: 25 minutes / servings: 4*

2½ pounds porterhouse steak	trim excess fat from the steak and pan-broil in a heavy
1 tablespoon butter	skillet to desired doneness. remove to a hot platter
1 teaspoon salt	
dash nutmeg	add 1 tablespoon of butter, salt, nutmeg, and mushrooms to the pan juices. sauté for 2
1 can mushrooms	minutes, then add the cream, and cook 2 minutes longer
2 tablespoons cream	
freshly ground pepper	pour the sauce over the steak and sprinkle lavishly with pepper

93

CUBE STEAKS,
COVENTRY STYLE *time: 15 minutes / servings: 4*

here is a good, quick way to make cheap cuts of steak taste like a million dollars

2 pounds cube steak, ¼-inch thick (about 8 steaks)

flour

salt

freshly ground pepper

2 tablespoons oil

1 cup chopped onions

2 tablespoons vinegar

1 tablespoon brown sugar

1 cup catsup

4 tablespoons Worcestershire sauce

1 cup cream

dredge the steaks in flour, season with salt and pepper, and brown quickly (about 1 minute on each side) in a heavy hot skillet containing 2 tablespoons oil. remove to a heated platter

reduce the heat, add the onions, then the remaining ingredients. simmer for 10 minutes. pour the sauce over the steaks, and serve

94

PAPRIKA MINUTE STEAK time: 15 minutes / servings: 2

1 pound minute or cube steak ½-inch thick	using a heavy hot skillet, brown the steak quickly in the butter and remove to a hot platter (10 minutes should do it)
4 tablespoons butter	
½ cup cream	
1 teaspoon paprika	reduce the heat and add the remaining ingredients to the skillet. simmer 2 minutes and pour over the steak
1 teaspoon lemon juice	
salt	
pepper	
dash Tabasco sauce	

STEAK, BUTTER-GIN FLAMBÉ time: 20 minutes / servings: 4

here is a quick, delicious way to serve almost any not-too-thick steak—exciting, too!

2½ pounds steak, 1-inch thick (almost any kind, if it's tender)	trim the excess fat from the steak and pan-broil in a heavy hot skillet to desired doneness
salt	season with salt and pepper and remove to a heated platter
freshly ground pepper	
3 tablespoons butter	add the butter to the skillet and brown slightly, add the gin and ignite
4 tablespoons gin	
	pour over the steak and serve while still blazing

95

OVEN-BROILED
STRIP STEAK time: 30 minutes / servings: 4

this is also variously known as a New York cut, a Kansas City steak, or a shell steak. the trick is that the tenderloin and tail have been removed—and sometimes the bone, too. call it what you will, this is one of the nicest morsels cut from the entire animal

2½ pounds Porterhouse steak with bone, tail, and tenderloin removed *1 clove garlic, cut* *salt*	rub the steak on both sides with cut garlic. place on the greased rack of a broiler pan and slide into preheated broiler, at high temperature, about 2 inches from the heat. leave the broiler door open
freshly ground pepper *1 tablespoon butter*	broil until top side is brown. season, turn, and repeat on other side
chopped parsley	serve on a heated platter or serving board. place butter beneath steak and garnish top with parsley

SLICED STEAK,
MUSTARD SAUCE *time: 25 minutes / servings: 4*

2 to 2¼ pounds flank steak

1 large onion, chopped

4 tablespoons butter

flour

3 tablespoons vinegar

1 teaspoon dry mustard

1 teaspoon paprika

½ teaspoon thyme

1 teaspoon salt

½ teaspoon pepper

½ teaspoon cayenne

1 cup water

cut the steak diagonally into ½-inch slices

brown the chopped onion in 2 tablespoons butter, using a heavy skillet

dredge the steak slices in flour and sauté them gently until brown on both sides

meanwhile, using a saucepan, melt 2 tablespoons butter, stir in the flour, and then the remaining ingredients. simmer about 5 minutes

pour the sauce over the steak slices, cover, simmer 5 minutes longer, and serve

97

GRILLED STEAK
ON SKEWERS *time: 20 minutes / servings: 6*

3 pounds boneless steak, cut into 1-inch cubes (any kind will do if it's tender)

arrange the cubes on skewers alternating each with an onion

20 small white onions

2 tablespoons olive oil containing a clove of garlic, minced

brush well with the garlic-oil, grill under the broiler for a few minutes until brown. turn often

season and serve

salt

pepper

these go well in the backyard, too, cooked over a bed of hot charcoal

---

CHATEAUBRIAND *time: 30 minutes / servings: 12 to 18*

the whole tenderloin is the most expensive part of the steer. it's all solid meat—no bone, no fat . . . no waste. weighing from 4 to 6 pounds, the tenderloin will serve a party of 12 to 18 hungry eaters in sumptuous style—and, believe it or not, in half an hour

have the tenderloin trimmed, tied, and larded (it's very lean meat, you know). sauté it 10 minutes in a very heavy hot skillet containing a couple tablespoons oil (olive oil, or butter and oil mixed fifty-fifty). turn it so that it will brown thoroughly on all sides
reduce the heat, cover, and cook 5 minutes longer
carve into thin slices, arrange overlapping on a hot platter, dot with butter, and garnish with minced parsley

Ground beef, chopped steak, hamburger—call it what you will—
it's the hurry-up cook's most constant friend. But even this old
friend can cross you up unless you're a careful, alert shopper
and know just what you want, because there are all kinds of
ground beef on the meat counters. There's ground meat that's
usually made up of a combination of beef, veal, and pork. And
there's ground beef (all beef). But this beef, itself, can come
from various cuts of the steer—from the round, or the sirloin tail,
or the rib, or the neck, or the chuck, or the flank. Or it can be
made up of a mixture of several cuts. If you want lean hamburger
(and there's nothing wrong with fat hamburger, except that you
usually end up with a skillet full of grease), you will buy ground
round or ground chuck.

Once you have bought your ground beef, the next step is up to
you. You can slap it into a hot skillet, cook it, and serve it. Or
you can add a pinch of imagination and a dash of daring and
enter an entire new hamburger world.

99

CHOPPED STEAK,
ROQUEFORT time: 20 to 25 minutes / servings: 4

*1½ pounds chopped chuck or
round*

2 tablespoons oil

*½ cup Roquefort cheese,
crumbled*

3 tablespoons butter

*1 tablespoon dry mustard
(or Dijon mustard)*

1 teaspoon salt

½ teaspoon pepper

form the meat into 8 patties
and brown quickly on both
sides in a heavy hot oiled
skillet

combine the remaining
ingredients and form into a
paste

spread over the meat patties,
cover the skillet, and cook
5 minutes longer or to
desired doneness

CHOPPED STEAK
DE LUXE *time: 20 to 25 minutes / servings: 4*

1 onion, chopped

*1 tablespoon chopped shallots
(or spring onions)*

dash Worcestershire

1 teaspoon dry mustard

2 teaspoons salt

freshly ground pepper

4 tablespoons butter

1 egg, lightly beaten

*1½ pounds chopped chuck or
round*

3 tablespoons sour cream

sauté the onion, shallots, and seasonings in 2 tablespoons butter for 2 minutes

add this mixture and the lightly beaten egg to the meat, blending well

form into four patties and broil on both sides to desired doneness in a heavy hot skillet with 2 tablespoons butter

remove to a heated platter and add the sour cream to the pan juices, simmer a minute or so, and pour over the steak patties

101

HAMBURGER GUMBO *time: 25 minutes / servings: 4 to 6*

1 pound hamburger, loose	cook-stir the hamburger and onions until hamburger is crumbly (about 5 minutes)
1 cup chopped onions	
1 can condensed chicken gumbo soup	add the remaining ingredients, mix well, cover, and cook 20 minutes
1 tablespoon catsup	
1 tablespoon prepared mustard	
1 teaspoon salt	
½ teaspoon pepper	

HAMBURGER CREOLE *time: 25 minutes / servings: 4*

3 slices bacon, chopped	sauté the bacon and onion until brown (about 2 minutes)
1 onion, chopped	
1 pound hamburger, loose	add the hamburger and cook —stir until brown (about 5 minutes)
½ cup diced celery	
¼ cup chopped green pepper	add the remaining ingredients, mix well, cover, and cook 15 minutes
2 tablespoons flour	
1 cup canned tomatoes	
1 teaspoon salt	

102

To defrost quick . . . place frozen food in the oven at 200°. The defrosting action is speeded up without cooking.

HAMBURGER, AS-YOU-LIKE-IT *time: 14 to 20 minutes / servings: 4*

1 pound hamburger, not too lean

1 teaspoon salt

½ teaspoon freshly ground pepper

form the hamburger into 4 patties about 1½ inches thick, season with salt and pepper, and broil in a heavy hot skillet until brown on the outside and pink inside (about 10 minutes)

remove to a heated platter and serve with a sauce made by stirring into the skillet juices . . .

2 tablespoons butter, 1 teaspoon prepared mustard, and 1 tablespoon chili sauce

or

2 tablespoons butter and 2 tablespoons chopped chives or onion

or

2 tablespoons butter and 2 tablespoons Roquefort cheese

or

2 tablespoons butter, ½ cup chopped canned mushrooms, ½ cup canned golden mushroom soup, and 2 teaspoons sherry

or

2 tablespoons butter, 1 tablespoon Worcestershire sauce, and ½ cup grated American cheese

or

2 tablespoons butter, ½ clove garlic (crushed), and 2 tablespoons tomato paste

103

CHOPPED STEAK
CAVALIER

time: 15 to 20 minutes / servings: 4

1 medium onion, finely chopped

1 tablespoon butter

1½ pounds chopped chuck or round

½ cup chopped parsley

2 eggs

2 slices white bread, crumbled

salt

pepper

sauté the onion in butter for 2 minutes using a small saucepan

mix the meat, parsley, eggs, and bread. season with salt and pepper and form into 4 patties

broil in a heavy saucepan, turn, cover with the sautéed onion, and continue cooking to desired doneness

104

FAKE STEAK *time: 10 to 14 minutes / servings: 4*

1 pound hamburger	mix all the ingredients and form into a steak about 1-inch thick. pat lightly between 2 pieces of waxed paper until firm and solid
½ cup milk	
1 teaspoon salt	
½ teaspoon pepper	broil quickly on both sides to desired doneness in a heavy hot skillet
2 tablespoons butter	

the "steak" should be brown and crusty on the outside and pink inside

remove to a heated platter. stir 2 tablespoons butter into the pan juices and pour over the meat

STEAK TARTARE *time: 13 minutes / servings: 4*

2 pounds lean steak, very finely ground (fillet mignon or top round)	mix chopped steak, egg yolks, chives, onion, and seasonings
4 raw egg yolks	spread mixture on bread slices, garnish with anchovies and capers
½ cup finely chopped chives	serve raw with lemon wedges
2 tablespoons finely chopped onion	
dash cayenne pepper	
1 teaspoon salt	
4 slices rye bread, buttered	
8 anchovy fillets	
2 tablespoons capers	
4 lemon wedges	

105

GERMAN MEATBALLS *time: 25 minutes / servings: 4*

½ pound hamburger

½ pound veal

1 cup cooked riced potatoes

1 tablespoon chopped canned anchovies

2 tablespoons chopped onion

1 teaspoon salt

½ teaspoon pepper

flour

1 cup chopped onions

2 tablespoons butter

2 tablespoons flour

½ teaspoon salt

1 tablespoon vinegar

2 cups water

mix the hamburger, veal, potatoes, anchovies, onion, and seasonings together. form into balls 1½ inches in diameter, roll in flour, and set aside

meanwhile sauté a cup of chopped onions in 2 tablespoons butter, add flour, salt, vinegar, and water. cook 5 minutes then add the meatballs and cook 15 minutes longer

HUNGARIAN
MEATBALLS *time: 25 to 30 minutes / servings: 4*

1 pound hamburger, ground twice

1 clove garlic, crushed

½ cup dry bread crumbs

2 teaspoons paprika

1 teaspoon salt

1 egg, slightly beaten

¼ cup milk

butter

½ cup canned chopped mushrooms

2 tablespoons flour

2 cups sour cream

2 tablespoons chopped parsley

mix the hamburger, garlic, bread crumbs, paprika, salt, egg, and milk together and form into balls 1½ inches in diameter

sauté in butter until golden (about 15 minutes) and remove to a heated platter

meanwhile combine mushrooms, flour, and sour cream. cook-stir until smooth and creamy (about 5 minutes)

pour the sauce over the meatballs and serve garnished with parsley

107

DANISH MEATBALLS   *time: 20 to 25 minutes / servings: 4*

½ *pound hamburger, ground twice*	mix the 2 meats together thoroughly
½ *pound lean pork, ground twice*	mix the flour, milk, and seasonings together
½ *cup flour*	combine the two mixtures and beat until light and fluffy (a blender will come in handy for this job)
1 cup milk	
1 teaspoon salt	
½ *teaspoon pepper*	form into balls about 1½ inches in diameter, and sauté in butter until golden (about 15 minutes)
4 tablespoons butter	

To retain the best flavor of canned vegetables . . . drain the liquid into a saucepan and reduce to half the quantity. Add the vegetables, heat quick, season and serve.

INDIAN MEATBALLS *time: 30 minutes / servings: 4*

1 pound hamburger	mix the hamburger, tomato paste, bread crumbs, salt, and ½ teaspoon curry powder together. form into balls 1½ inches in diameter
½ cup tomato paste	
½ cup dry bread crumbs	
½ teaspoon salt	sauté in oil until brown (about 6 minutes) and set aside
½ teaspoon curry powder	
2 tablespoons oil	to the skillet juices stir in the bouillon, onion, raisins, 1 teaspoon curry powder, ginger, and salt. simmer 5 minutes, then thicken with 1 tablespoon flour mixed with ½ cup water
1 cup beef bouillon	
2 tablespoons chopped onion	
½ cup seedless raisins	
1 teaspoon curry powder	return the meatballs to the skillet and simmer 5 minutes longer. serve with rice
pinch ginger	
1 teaspoon salt	
1 tablespoon flour	
½ cup water	

ITALIAN MEATBALLS *time: 20 to 25 minutes / servings: 4*

1 pound hamburger

1 clove garlic, crushed

½ teaspoon orégano

mix the hamburger, garlic, seasonings, and egg together. form into balls 1½ inches in diameter, roll in bread crumbs and cheese

1 teaspoon salt

½ teaspoon pepper

sauté in hot oil until golden (about 10 minutes)

serve with spaghetti (canned, or see index)

1 egg, slightly beaten

½ cup dry bread crumbs

½ cup grated Parmesan cheese

2 tablespoons olive oil

MEXICAN MEATBALLS *time: 30 minutes / servings: 4*

½ pound hamburger	mix the hamburger, pork, onion, salt, and pepper together. form into balls 1½ inches in diameter and roll in bread crumbs
½ pound ground lean pork	
1 onion, chopped	
1 teaspoon salt	sauté in hot oil until golden (about 10 minutes) and remove to a heated platter
½ teaspoon pepper	
½ cup dry bread crumbs	to the skillet juices add the garlic, onion, green pepper, chili powder, tomato paste, and water. cook-stir for 10 minutes and pour over the meatballs
2 tablespoons olive oil	
1 clove garlic, crushed	
1 onion, chopped	
½ cup chopped green pepper	
1 teaspoon chili powder	
½ cup tomato paste	
1 cup water	

SWEDISH
MEATBALLS *time: 25 to 30 minutes / servings: 4*

½ pound hamburger, ground twice

½ pound pork, ground twice

½ cup finely chopped onion

1 teaspoon salt

½ teaspoon pepper

pinch allspice

1 egg, slightly beaten and mixed with 1 cup milk

2 cups bread crumbs

2 tablespoons fat

1 can beef bouillon

mix the hamburger, pork, onion, and seasonings together, form into balls about 1-inch in diameter. soak in the egg-milk mixture for a minute or so

roll in bread crumbs and brown in hot fat for about 5 minutes

add a can of beef bouillon, cover, and cook 10 minutes longer

"Water is the only liquid drunk by the animals, whereas man demands more from a drink than a simple quenching of thirst," *Larousse Gastronomique.*

112

QUICK MEAT LOAF *time: 30 minutes / servings: 4*

this is one of America's favorite dinner dishes. but, requiring an hour or more in the oven plus additional time for preparation, meat loaf does not as a rule qualify for inclusion among quick dishes. but rules don't count when my wife is fixing dinner in a hurry. you need a meat loaf in half an hour, that's what you'll get—and there'll be no sacrifices to quality, or taste, or enjoyment. try this quick top-of-the-stove meat loaf of hers and you'll see. chances are you'll never go back to the oven again

½ pound ground beef	mix all the ingredients (except the bacon) and form into an oval loaf about 2 inches thick
½ pound ground pork	
½ cup bread crumbs	
1 egg, lightly beaten	fry the bacon for 2 minutes in a heavy skillet and remove
1 tablespoon minced onion (fresh, frozen, or dried)	place the loaf into the skillet and lay the half-cooked bacon strips over the top. cover tightly and cook over medium heat about 20 minutes or until loaf is browned and bacon is crisp, basting occasionally
¼ cup milk	
½ teaspoon salt	
¼ teaspoon freshly ground pepper	
4 strips bacon	serve with pan gravy or, if you prefer, with mushroom sauce (see index)

if there are only two of you, there'll be enough left over for tomorrow. serve it cold . . . mmm!

PRESSURE-COOKER
CHILI CON CARNE *time: 30 minutes / servings: 4 to 6*

chili con carne is not a dish you usually cook in a hurry—often it's set on the back burner to simmer all day. you'll find yourself hard pressed to overcook chili. but in this book we're talking about quick cooking, so get out the old pressure cooker and follow along. you'll be surprised what you can come up with in half an hour. suggestion: double the quantities given below and make enough for tomorrow. chili is always better the second day

3 tablespoons olive oil	put the oil, garlic, and onions into the pressure cooker and brown 2 minutes
2 cloves garlic, crushed	
2 cups chopped onions	stir in the beef and brown 10 minutes longer
2 pounds lean beef, cubed or chopped	add the seasonings and bouillon, adjust the cover, bring to 15 pounds pressure, and cook 15 minutes
4 tablespoons chili powder	
1 teaspoon orégano	reduce the pressure, remove the cover, and serve in bowls mixed with hot kidney beans (you control the hotness by adding more, or less, bean juice)
1 teaspoon cumin	
½ teaspoon cayenne pepper	
1 teaspoon salt	
2 cups beef bouillon	
1 or 2 cans kidney beans	

HALF-HOUR
GOULASH   *time: 30 minutes / servings: 2*

goulash, a middle European version of stew, can be made in the pressure cooker under the same specifications and following the same time schedule as Half-hour Beef Stew. the following recipe provides dinner for 2. it'll take a few minutes longer to make double the quantity

1 pound boneless beef or veal (or both)	cut the meat into ½-inch cubes and season with salt
1 teaspoon salt	put the pressure cooker onto the stove at high heat and
4 slices bacon, cut into pieces	toss in the bacon, onions, garlic, and paprika
1 cup frozen (or fresh) chopped onions	dredge the meat cubes with flour, adding them to the hot
1 clove garlic, chopped	pot as you go
3 teaspoons paprika	brown the meat on all sides for about 5 minutes, then
flour	pour in the water and wine. adjust the cover, bring to 15
½ cup hot water	pounds pressure, and cook for 15 minutes
½ cup dry red wine	reduce the pressure, stir in the cream and serve on hot
½ cup sour cream	noodles
2 cups cooked noodles	

115

HALF-HOUR
BEEF STEW   *time: 30 minutes / servings: 2*

indisputably, food prepared in a pressure cooker lacks something in flavor, comes out with all the ingredients tasting alike. there's a lot to be said in favor of slow cooking over low heat—for a long time. but if time is a factor in your culinary day, you could go a long time without serving stew or goulash. the often-maligned pressure cooker can fix all that. here's the proof—and with it—a step-by-step time schedule to help you make the half hour deadline:

INGREDIENTS	TIME	STEP	PROCEDURE
1 pound boneless beef stew meat	−30 min	(1)	cut the beef into ½-inch cubes and season well with salt and pepper
salt			
pepper		(2)	put the pressure cooker on the stove at high heat, and add the oil
2 tablespoons oil			
flour			
1 cup frozen (or fresh) chopped onions		(3)	dredge the beef cubes with flour, tossing them into the hot pot as you go
½ cup hot water		(4)	brown the beef on all sides, while you add the chopped onions
½ cup dry red wine			
2 medium potatoes	−20 min	(5)	pour in the water and wine, cover, bring to 15 pounds pressure, then reduce the heat
2 small carrots			
		(6)	peel and cut 2 poatoes and 2 small carrots into 1-inch cubes
		(7)	start setting the table

116

−10 min	(8)	reduce the pressure quickly (run cold water onto the cooker), add the vegetables, cover, and bring back to 15 pounds
	(9)	finish setting the table
−0 min	(10)	the stew is done. reduce the pressure, remove the cover, and serve (or turn off the heat and allow pressure to subside gradually until you're ready to serve)

you have just produced a beautiful, flavorful stew with tender meat and vegetables cooked just right. and what's more, the gravy is exactly the right thickness, too. while you're at it, it won't take but a few minutes longer to make enough for tomorrow. reheated stew is the most!

BEEF STROGONOFF   *time: 20 minutes / servings: 4*

*2 pounds boneless steak,
¼-inch thick, sliced into
1-inch strips (almost any kind
will do if it's tender)*

1 teaspoon salt

*½ teaspoon freshly ground
pepper*

1 teaspoon paprika

2 tablespoons butter

1 onion, grated

1 tablespoon flour

*1 cup beef stock (or
consommé)*

1 cup sour cream

1 teaspoon chopped parsley

season the steak slices with salt, pepper, and paprika. place them in a skillet with 1 tablespoon of the butter and the grated onion. broil gently for 2 minutes on each side

using a second skillet, melt 1 tablespoon butter and stir in the flour and then the stock. simmer 2 minutes, then add the sour cream

add the steak slices and pan juices and cook 5 minutes longer. serve garnished with chopped parsley

CREAMED CHIPPED
BEEF *time: 20 minutes / servings: 2*

¼ *pound package chipped beef*

4 tablespoons butter

3 tablespoons flour

2 cups milk

3 slices buttered toast

separate the slices of beef, tear into pieces and discard any stringy bits

melt the butter in a skillet, add the beef, sprinkle with flour, and stir in 2 cups milk. cook-stir over low heat until thickened

serve on toast (or cooked rice)

frankfurters are, without a doubt, the number one quick dish. already cooked, they need only a little heating in order to make them palatable. you can serve them boiled, pan-broiled, or grilled —plain and simple, or fancied up

FRANKFURTERS
WITH CHEESE

try slitting frankfurters, inserting a sliver of cheese, and broiling them slit side up until the cheese melts

119

FRANKFURTERS
WITH BACON

or wrap frankfurters in slices of bacon (with or without the cheese) and fasten with toothpicks. grill until bacon is cooked

FRANKFURTERS
WITH CHILI

or broil split frankfurters and serve them on rolls or toast covered with canned chili and chopped onions. (you might wish to hot up the chili a little. add a teaspoon of chili powder and a dash of Tabasco sauce, and cook for 5 minutes)

Augment a simple dinner quick by starting off with a cup of canned soup, hot or cold. Be inventive. Blend different soups or add garnishes.

FRANKFURTERS
SOUTHERN STYLE *time: 30 minutes / servings: 4*

1 onion, chopped

½ cup chopped celery

½ green pepper, chopped

1 tablespoon bacon fat

*1 pound frankfurters, cut into
pieces*

1 large can tomatoes

pinch thyme

pinch orégano

1 teaspoon salt

dash Tabasco sauce

6 slices buttered toast

using a medium saucepan,
sauté the onion, celery, and
green pepper in bacon fat for
about 10 minutes

add the frankfurters,
tomatoes, and seasonings

cover and simmer over low
heat for 15 minutes

serve on buttered toast (or
with cooked rice)

121

VEAL CUTLETS

veal cutlets, we call them. in Italy they say *scaloppine,* in the Middle European countries they're *schnitzel.* they all start (or should) with a ⅜-inch thick slice of the round (called by the French *plume de veau*) which you pound to a thickness of ¼-inch but be careful when you buy, many stores sell just any old cut of veal sliced thin and call it veal cutlets. yours should be free from muscle, gristle, or striations

a really great quick dish, these little morsels can be prepared in an endless variety of ways, and all in a very short time

SCALOPPINE
ALLA MILANESE *time: 18 minutes / servings: 4*

*1½ pounds veal cutlets,
⅜-inch thick, pounded to
¼-inch*

salt

pepper

½ cup flour

2 eggs, beaten

1 cup bread crumbs

½ cup butter

½ cup olive oil

4 lemon slices

chopped parsley

season the cutlets with salt and pepper, dredge with flour, dip in egg, and then in bread crumbs

heat the butter and oil in a heavy skillet and put in the cutlets. turn almost at once and sauté over low heat for 5 minutes. turn again and cook for 5 minutes longer or until crisp and golden

serve at once garnished with parsley and lemon slices

123

SCALOPPINE ALLA
BOLOGNESE *time: 20 minutes / servings: 4*

*1½ pounds veal cutlets,
⅜-inch thick, pounded to
¼-inch*

1 cup butter

grated Parmesan cheese

2 tablespoons Marsala wine

*4 tablespoons beef or
chicken stock*

sauté the cutlets in butter over low heat about 5 minutes on each side or until crisp and golden. remove to a heated platter and cover with Parmesan cheese

stir the wine and stock into the pan juices and simmer a couple of minutes

pour the pan juices over the cutlets and cheese, and serve at once

SCALOPPINE AL
MARSALA *time: 20 minutes / servings: 4*

prepare *Scaloppine alla Bolognese* (above) omitting the cheese

124

SCALOPPINE
PARMIGIANA *time: 25 minutes / servings: 4*

4 slices (about 1½ pounds) veal cutlets, ⅜-inch thick, pounded to ¼-inch	rub the cutlets well with cut garlic, and season with salt and pepper
1 clove garlic, cut	dip the cutlets into egg, then into bread crumbs, then into the grated cheese
1 teaspoon salt	
½ teaspoon pepper	heat the oil in a heavy skillet and put in the cutlets. sauté 5 minutes on each side
2 eggs, lightly beaten	
dry bread crumbs	place a slice of Mozzarella cheese on each cutlet, top with tomato purée, and brown under the broiler for a minute or so
½ cup grated Parmesan cheese	
½ cup olive oil	
4 slices Mozzarella cheese	
½ cup tomato purée	

SCHNITZEL, NATUR   *time: 15 minutes / servings: 4*

1½ pounds veal cutlets, ⅜-inch thick, pounded to ¼-inch	season the cutlets with paprika, salt, and cayenne, and dust very lightly with flour
1 teaspoon paprika	
1 teaspoon salt	heat the butter in a heavy skillet and sauté the cutlets 3 or 4 minutes on each side
few grains cayenne pepper	until crisp and golden
flour	remove to a heated platter
3 tablespoons butter	add ½ cup water to the skillet juices, cook-stir for a minute
½ cup water	or so, and pour over the schnitzel

SCHNITZEL À LA HOLSTEIN   *time: 20 to 25 minutes / servings: 4*

prepare *schnitzel natur* and serve with a fried egg and anchovy fillets on each schnitzel. garnish with capers and a slice of lemon or dredge the cutlets with flour, dip them in egg, and then bread crumbs, sauté, and serve with a fried egg and anchovies on top of each

BROILED LAMB
CHOPS OR STEAKS

place chops or steaks on a greased broiler rack and grill 2 inches from the heat in a preheated broiler half the prescribed time, turn, and complete the cooking on the other side. season, dot with butter, and serve. depending upon how rare or well-done you like them, chops 1-inch thick require 12 to 15 minutes total time, 1½ inches thick about 20 minutes

pan-broiling takes less time. use a heavy skillet and pour off the juices as they accumulate

LAMB PATTIES *time: 20 minutes / servings: 4*

1½ *pounds ground lamb*	form the lamb into 4 flat patties and season with salt and pepper
salt	
pepper	wrap each with 2 slices bacon and fasten with toothpicks
8 *slices bacon*	
	broil in a heavy skillet about 10 minutes, turning often

MIXED GRILL *time: 16 minutes / servings: 2*

2 *1-inch thick lamb chops*	place the chops, kidneys, and sausages on a greased broiler rack
2 *kidneys, split*	
4 *small pork sausages, parboiled 3 minutes*	slide into the broiler 2 inches from the heat and grill for 7 minutes
4 *strips bacon*	
1 *tomato, cut in half*	turn the chops, kidneys, and sausages, and add the bacon, tomato halves, and mushrooms. brush with melted butter, season with salt and pepper and broil 7 minutes longer
4 *medium mushroom caps*	
melted butter	
salt	
pepper	

128

HALF-HOUR
LAMB STEW *time: 30 minutes / servings: 2*

the problem with lamb is the fat. in slow-cooking, the fat can always be skimmed off as it rises to the top, but when you use a pressure cooker, the fat just accumulates unchecked. so for Half-hour Lamb Stew, you'll just have to start with lean lamb

2 tablespoons oil	put the pressure cooker onto the stove at high heat, add the oil and onions
1 cup frozen (or fresh) chopped onions	
1 pound boneless lamb, very lean	cut the lamb into 1-inch cubes, season with salt and pepper, and dredge with flour, and toss into the hot pot as you go
1 teaspoon salt	
½ teaspoon pepper	brown the lamb on all sides for about 5 minutes, then pour in the water, bring to a boil, adjust the cover, bring to 15 pounds pressure, and cook for 10 minutes
flour	
1 cup hot water	
½ cup cubed potato	reduce the pressure quickly, add the vegetables, cook for 10 minutes longer at 15 pounds pressure
½ cup cubed carrot	
1 cup cubed turnip	

129

BROILED PORK
CHOPS

fresh pork is a fine-grained and firm meat and requires more cooking than most other meats. it therefore lends itself only limitedly to quick preparation. pork chops cut thinly enough (1-inch thick or less) can be pan-broiled in less than half an hour. the trick is to brown them quickly on both sides in a heavy skillet, reduce the heat, cover the skillet, and continue cooking until tender (about 15 minutes)

PRESSURE-COOKER
PORK CHOPS *time: 28 minutes / servings: 2*

4 pork chops (about 1½ pounds)	brown the chops (about 3 minutes on each side) in hot oil in an uncovered pressure cooker, season with salt and pepper
2 tablespoons cooking oil	
¼ cup water	place a rack under the chops, add ¼ cup water, cover, bring to 15 pounds pressure, and cook for 15 minutes
salt	
pepper	
1 tablespoon flour mixed in ½ cup water	reduce the pressure, remove the chops, thicken the gravy with the floured water, and serve

BROILED PORK
TENDERLOIN *time: 26 minutes / servings: 4*

4 slices fresh pork tenderloin (about 1½ pounds), cut into ½-inch slices

pound the pork slices to about ¼-inch thick, brush with melted butter, and brown for 3 minutes on each side in a heavy hot skillet

melted butter

salt

pepper

reduce the heat, cover the skillet, and slow-cook until tender (about 15 minutes)

season to taste with salt and pepper and serve with the pan juices

(or stir a bit of flour into the skillet, add a little water, and make a thick gravy)

131

PAN-BROILED
LIVER WITH BACON *time: 10 minutes / servings: 4*

4 slices bacon	broil the bacon in a heavy skillet until crisp. remove the bacon and discard most of the fat
flour	
salt	
	flour and season the liver slightly and broil in the remaining fat, turning frequently (overcooking toughens the liver)
pepper	
1 pound liver, cut into 4 slices about ½-inch thick (calf's liver is best, but young beef, pork, or lamb liver is good, too)	serve with a piece of crisp bacon on each slice

SAUTÉED
SWEETBREADS *time: 25 minutes / servings: 4*

sweetbreads are a tender and delicate food, quick to cook, delicious to eat. veal sweetbreads are the best—and the most expensive—but lamb and young beef sweetbreads are good, too. one problem: before they can be cooked, there are a membrane and a couple of dark tubes that need removing. you can ease this job by simmering in salted water for 10 minutes

132

1 pound sweetbreads, prepared as above	melt the butter in a skillet and sauté the sweetbreads over medium heat until brown on all sides (about 10 minutes)
2 tablespoons butter	
salt	
	season to taste and serve on buttered toast with a lemon slice on each portion
4 slices buttered toast	
4 slices lemon	

PAN-BROILED
HAM STEAK *time: 10 minutes / servings: 2*

1 slice ham, ¾-inch thick
(about 1 pound)

slash the fat edges of the steak to prevent curling, place into a greased skillet, and cook 3 minutes

1 tablespoon oil

4 slices pineapple

turn and spread with a thick layer of brown sugar, broil 3 minutes longer, and remove to a heated platter

brown sugar

add the pineapple slices to the sugar and sauté briefly, taking care not to scorch the sugar

serve the ham topped with pineapple slices and a little of the juices

133

BROILED
SWEETBREADS   *time: 20 minutes / servings: 4*

1 pound sweetbreads	remove the membrane and tubes from the sweetbreads
2 tablespoons melted butter	and split. brush with melted butter, and grill for 3
salt	minutes in a preheated broiler 2 inches from the heat
pepper	turn, brush with butter again, and grill 2 minutes longer

QUICK CREAMED
SWEETBREADS
WITH MUSHROOMS   *time: 20 minutes / servings: 4*

1 pound sweetbreads	remove the membrane and tubes from the sweetbreads, cut them into small pieces, and place into a saucepan
1 can cream of mushroom soup	
salt	add the mushroom soup, season with salt and pepper, and cook 5 minutes
pepper	
4 slices buttered toast	serve on buttered toast points or in patty shells, dust with paprika
paprika	

134

SWEETBREADS
EN BROCHETTE *time: 25 minutes / servings: 4*

1 pound sweetbreads	remove the membrane and tubes from the sweetbreads and cut into cubes and thread on skewers alternating with bits of bacon
4 slices bacon, cut into squares	
2 tablespoons melted butter	
salt	brush with melted butter, season with salt and pepper, and sprinkle with bread crumbs
pepper	
½ cup bread crumbs	grill in the broiler 3 inches from the heat about 10 minutes or until bacon is crisp, turning to brown evenly

A quick way to handle brussels sprouts is to open the window and throw them out.

PAN-BROILED
KIDNEYS *time: 15 minutes / servings: 4*

8 *lamb kidneys (or 4 veal kidneys)*	remove white fat and tubes, cut the kidneys into ¼-inch slices, and season with salt
salt	and pepper
pepper	melt the butter in a heavy skillet, broil the kidneys
2 *tablespoons butter*	quickly until tender (about 5 minutes), and remove to a
2 *tablespoons dry red wine (or sherry)*	heated platter
	stir a little wine into the pan juices, bring to a boil, and pour over the kidneys

you might wish to add a few sliced mushrooms to the pan to cook along with the kidneys, in which case you should add a little extra butter

---

To combat gastronomic boredom, vary the kind of bread you serve. Switch about from French or Italian bread to muffins, rolls, or corn bread.

BROILED KIDNEYS
WITH BACON *time: 20 minutes / servings: 4*

2 lamb kidneys (or 4 veal kidneys)

remove the white fat and tubes from the kidneys and split them, cutting almost through. run a skewer through them laterally so that they remain flat and open

2 tablespoons melted butter

1 tablespoon lemon juice

salt

cayenne pepper

brush with melted butter and lemon juice, season with salt and cayenne, and wrap with bacon strips

4 slices bacon, cut in half

grill under the broiler 2 inches from the heat for 10 minutes or less (overcooking toughens kidneys)

4 slices buttered toast

serve on buttered toast

137

BEEF KIDNEY STEW *time: 25 minutes / servings: 4*

beef kidneys, less tender than those of lamb or veal, can stew a long time before they're ready to serve—unless you use a pressure cooker

1½ pounds beef kidneys	cut away the white fat parts of the kidneys, and dredge
flour	with flour
4 slices bacon, cut into pieces	using a pressure cooker, sauté the bacon, add the onion and
½ cup chopped onion (fresh or frozen)	garlic and cook until golden
½ clove garlic, chopped	add the kidneys, seasonings, wine, and consommé
½ teaspoon salt	cover, bring the pressure up to 15 pounds and cook 15
½ teaspoon pepper	minutes
½ cup dry red wine (or ¼ cup Madeira or sherry)	reduce the pressure, thicken the stew with a little flour and water if necessary,
can beef consommé	and serve

VEAL KIDNEY STEW *time: 25 minutes / servings: 4*

1½ pounds veal (or lamb) kidneys	cut away white fat parts of the kidneys, slice into ½-inch pieces, and dredge with flour
flour	
4 slices bacon, cut into pieces	sauté the bacon, add the onion and garlic, and cook until golden
¼ cup chopped onion (frozen chopped onion is quicker)	add the kidneys, salt, peppercorns, and consommé. cover and cook for 10 minutes longer
½ clove garlic, chopped	
½ teaspoon salt	add the wine, cover, and cook for 5 minutes longer
a few peppercorns	
1 can beef consommé	
½ cup dry red wine (or ¼ cup Madeira or sherry mixed with ¼ cup water)	

TRIPE AND ONIONS *time: 15 minutes / servings: 4*

2 tablespoons chopped onion	cook the onion in the butter for 5 minutes, add the tripe and seasonings, and cook for 5 minutes longer
2 tablespoons butter	
1½ pounds canned cooked tripe, cut into 2-inch squares	serve garnished with crumbled bacon and parsley
salt	
pepper	
3 slices bacon, cooked and crumbled	
chopped parsley	

139

BROILED TRIPE   *time: 13 minutes / servings: 4*

fresh tripe takes too long to cook to be included in a quick cookbook, but good honeycomb tripe is available in cans to satisfy the palate of those who love it

1½ pounds canned cooked tripe	cut the tripe into serving-size pieces, brush with olive oil, dredge with cracker dust, and season with salt and pepper
olive oil	
cracker dust	place the tripe on a broiler rack and grill 2 inches from the heat for about 10 minutes, turning after 5 minutes
salt	
pepper	
butter	serve, honeycomb-side up, dotted with butter

good with bacon and/or broiled tomato halves, too

7

FULL-MEAL SANDWICHES

Everybody knows how to make a sandwich. You butter two slices of bread and put something in between them—easy. But there are sandwiches . . . and sandwiches. We include a few in this book that might well be classified as losers—eat one and you lose your appetite.

DANISH OPEN
SANDWICHES

cover toasted, buttered French bread with hot scrambled eggs and chopped chives

cover toasted, buttered English muffins with hot scrambled eggs and anchovies

cover toasted, buttered rye bread with smoked salmon and hot scrambled eggs

cover toasted, buttered French bread with sardines, sliced tomatoes, and sliced stuffed olives

cover toasted, buttered English muffins with Roquefort cheese and sautéed chopped beef (loose)

cover toasted, buttered rye bread with raw filet mignon (ground three times), caviar, and chopped hard-cooked eggs

143

WESTERN SANDWICH

time: 10 minutes / servings: 1

1 tablespoon chopped onion

1 tablespoon chopped green pepper

1 teaspoon butter

1 egg, slightly beaten

1 tablespoon milk

1 tablespoon crumbled crisp bacon (or chopped ham)

2 slices buttered toasted bread (or a toasted roll)

using a heavy skillet, sauté the onion and green pepper in the butter for 5 minutes

combine the egg, milk, and bacon and add to the skillet. stir, then cook until omelet is golden on the bottom. turn and cook a moment on the other side

serve between two slices of toasted bread or in a toasted roll

WELSH SANDWICH WITH TOMATO SAUCE *time: 10 minutes / servings: 2*

1 cup canned tomatoes	make a sauce by combining the first 6 ingredients, bring to a boil, then simmer gently for 8 minutes
4 tablespoons chopped onion	
1 tablespoon chopped green pepper	meanwhile, toast the bread, butter it, place a slice of cheese on each, and grill under the broiler until cheese melts
¼ teaspoon salt	
½ teaspoon dry mustard	
dash Worcestershire	serve with the sauce poured over each sandwich
1 tablespoon butter	
2 slices French bread	
2 slices sharp Cheddar cheese	

FRIED SANDWICHES

put sliced or chopped chicken, ham, beef, or pork between two slices of bread. combine a slightly beaten egg and ¼ cup milk, season with salt and pepper, dip the sandwich into the mixture, and sauté on both sides in butter. (the mixture will be enough for 2 sandwiches.) serve garnished with sliced olives or crisp bacon

145

SLOPPY JOE
SANDWICHES   *time: 20 minutes / servings: 4*

½ *cup chopped onion*

½ *cup chopped green pepper*

2 tablespoons oil

*1½ pounds ground chuck
(or round)*

*1 tomato, peeled, squeezed,
and chopped*

1 teaspoon paprika

dash Worcestershire

1 teaspoon salt

4 hamburger rolls

using a heavy skillet, sauté
the onion and green pepper
in the oil until slightly brown

add the remaining ingredients
including the meat (loose)

cook over low heat 15
minutes, stirring often

spoon onto warm hamburger
rolls and serve

OPEN INTERNATIONAL CLUB
time: 10 minutes / servings: 4

¼ cup mayonnaise	mix the mayonnaise, relish, and onion and spread onto the bread slices
1 teaspoon pickle relish	
1 teaspoon chopped onion	cover each slice with 2 slices salami, 2 slices tomato, 1 slice turkey, and 1 slice cheese
4 large slices French bread	
8 slices hard salami	sprinkle with orégano and grill under the broiler at low heat until cheese melts
8 slices tomato	
4 slices cold turkey (or chicken)	
4 slices Swiss cheese	
orégano	

PHONY CHILI SANDWICHES
time: 12 minutes / servings: 2

1 tablespoon olive oil	mix all the ingredients and sauté in a hot skillet for 10 minutes
½ pound ground beef	
1 tablespoon chopped onion	serve between slices of heated rolls
¼ teaspoon orégano	
¼ teaspoon cumin seed	
1 teaspoon chili powder	
dash Tabasco	
2 large rolls	

147

HEROS *time: 10 minutes / servings: 2*

3 tablespoons butter	cream the butter and garlic
½ clove garlic, crushed	split the bread and spread both sides generously with the garlic butter
2 6-inch lengths of French bread	
6 canned pimentos	into each buttered sandwich insert 3 pimentos, 3 slices salami, 2 slices ham, and 3 slices cheese
6 slices Italian salami	
4 slices boiled ham	brush with olive oil, close, and eat!
6 slices cheese (provolone or Swiss)	
olive oil	

FAKE PIZZAS *time: 5 minutes / servings: 2*

2 English muffins, split and toasted	spread the English muffin halves generously with marinara sauce, cover with slices of cheese, and sprinkle with orégano
canned marinara spaghetti sauce	
4 slices Mozzarella cheese	slide under the broiler and cook until the cheese melts
½ teaspoon orégano	

8

SALADS

The basic salad consists of raw greens tossed with oil and vinegar (French dressing). The greens may be any variety of lettuce (iceberg, Boston, romaine, escarole, chicory, bibb, etc.), watercress, endive, dandelion greens, spinach. . . . And you can combine varieties of greens as you wish.

To make a good salad, you wash the greens in cold water, shake off most of the wetness, then dry each leaf thoroughly with a towel. Break into bite-size pieces.

Put the greens into a salad bowl (previously rubbed with garlic, if you wish), pour on the French dressing, and toss until each leaf is well coated and no dressing remains in the bottom of the bowl. Season to taste, as you toss, with salt and pepper—and with whatever chopped herbs you might want (chives, parsley, chervil, tarragon, etc.).

You can garnish this basic salad with all kinds of good things and build it into a complete meal using, for instance, radishes, olives, sliced tomatoes, onions, cucumber, or carrots; chopped celery, hard-cooked eggs, or bacon; julienne ham, chicken, or turkey; or croûtons fried in bacon fat.

BASIC FRENCH
DRESSING

mix 3 parts olive oil with 1 part vinegar or lemon juice. vary the proportions to make more, or less, tart according to your taste

ROQUEFORT OR
BLUE CHEESE
DRESSING

to basic French dressing, add crumbled Roquefort or blue cheese and a little cream or mayonnaise

THOUSAND ISLAND
DRESSING

to basic French dressing, add onion juice, paprika, chopped parsley, sliced stuffed olives, a little Worcestershire sauce and a little dry or prepared mustard

HERB DRESSING

to basic French dressing, add a little finely crushed dried marjoram and chopped parsley. season with a few drops Worcestershire or A-1 sauce

151

RUSSIAN DRESSING

mix together equal parts of mayonnaise and chili sauce, add a little relish, and season to taste

GERMAN POTATO
SALAD time: 15 minutes / servings: 2

1 medium onion, chopped

1 tablespoon cooking oil

1 tablespoon flour

2 tablespoons sugar

2 tablespoons vinegar

4 tablespoons water

salt

pepper

¼ cup chopped celery

1 tablespoon chopped parsley

*3 frankfurters, cooked
and chopped*

2 cups hot diced potatoes

fry the onion in the oil until golden, and blend in the flour

add the sugar, vinegar, water, and seasonings. cook for 1 minute

add the celery and parsley, and cook for 1 minute longer

add the frankfurters and potatoes, heat, and stir. serve hot

AVOCADO SALAD   *time: 5 minutes / servings: 2*

split an avocado, remove the seed, fill with French dressing (see index) and serve on lettuce leaves. or stuff with fresh, cooked (or frozen or canned) shrimp, crab meat, or lobster topped with mayonnaise. or use chopped cooked chicken

CHEF'S SALAD

this can be a mixture of almost anything. here is the classic recipe: start with a basic salad, add julienne turkey, ham, tongue, and Swiss cheese, toss in a few olives, a quartered tomato, a quartered hard-cooked egg, and a few capers. Pour on your favorite dressing, toss . . . and you'll have a real meal-in-itself salad that will please everybody

SEAFOOD SALAD

mix cooked fresh, frozen, or canned seafood (such as lobster meat, crab meat, shrimp, salmon, or tuna) with mayonnaise and serve on a bed of lettuce leaves. garnish with capers, sliced hard-cooked eggs, or tomatoes

A quick and delicious way to top off a meal: serve a variety of cheeses with toasted crackers.

153

CRAB MEAT LOUIS *time: 5 minutes / servings: 4*

lettuce leaves	shred the lettuce and spoon on the crab meat
2 cups cooked fresh (or frozen or canned) crab meat	mix the remaining ingredients and pour over the crab meat
½ cup French dressing (see index)	
2 tablespoons mayonnaise	
⅓ cup chili sauce	
dash Worcestershire	
salt	
pepper	

WALDORF SALAD *time: 10 minutes / servings: 2 or 3*

lettuce leaves	tear the lettuce into bite-size bits, place in the salad bowl and season with salt and pepper
salt	
pepper	
2 cups diced apples	add the remaining ingredients, toss, and serve
1 cup diced celery	
½ cup mayonnaise	
chopped walnuts	

DE LUXE CHICKEN SALAD *time: 15 minutes / servings: 2 or 3*

lettuce leaves	tear the lettuce leaves into bite-size bits, place into the salad bowl with French dressing, and toss
½ cup French dressing (see index)	
2 cups diced cooked chicken	add the remaining ingredients, toss again, and serve
1 cup chopped celery	
1 cup mayonnaise	
1 hard-cooked egg, sliced	
2 tablespoons capers	

155

CAESAR SALAD *time: 12 minutes / servings: 2*

1 head romaine lettuce	tear the lettuce into bite-size bits, place into the salad bowl and sprinkle with salt, freshly ground pepper, and grated cheese
salt	
freshly ground pepper	
¼ cup grated Parmesan cheese	squeeze the juice from 1 lemon onto the greens and pour on the garlic-flavored oil and a few drops Worcestershire sauce
1 lemon	
¼ cup olive oil containing ½ clove garlic, crushed	break an egg over the salad, toss, add the croûtons, toss again, and taste for seasoning
Worcestershire sauce	
1 egg	
½ cup croûtons	

156

9
SAUCES

A good sauce often spells the difference between an ordinary everyday dish and one that will make your palate sit up and say ahh.

There are many reasonably good sauces available commercially, but there is no sauce like the one you, yourself, have made just for the occasion. If time places limitations on the elaborateness of some preparations, there are still others that can be made quickly while the main dinner dish is cooking. In some cases, you might find an electric blender a blessing.

BECHAMEL SAUCE (BASIC WHITE SAUCE) *time: 12 minutes / yield: 2 cups*

4 tablespoons butter	put all the ingredients into the container of an electric blender and blend for half a minute at full speed
1 teaspoon salt	
pinch pepper	
4 tablespoons flour	pour into saucepan and cook over low heat for 10 minutes, stirring constantly
2 cups hot milk	

to make a thicker sauce, use 6 tablespoons flour instead of 4; mixing the milk fifty-fifty with cream will make a richer sauce. if you don't have a blender, do the whole job in the saucepan, mixing the flour, butter, and seasonings first, then stirring in the milk. keep the heat low or the flour will brown. time (without a blender): about 20 minutes

EGG SAUCE *time: 15 to 25 minutes / yield: 3 cups*

to basic white sauce, add 3 hard-cooked eggs, finely chopped

CURRY SAUCE *time: 12 to 20 minutes / yielu. 2 cups*

to basic white sauce, add, before cooking, 1 teaspoon curry powder

159

HERB SAUCE *time: 14 to 22 minutes / yiel*
2 cups

to basic white sauce, add 1 tablespoon chopped fresh herb. (or
½ tablespoon dried herbs), such as parsley, chives, dill

MUSHROOM SAUCE *time: 14 to 22 minutes / yield:*
2½ cups

to basic white sauce, add ½ cup finely chopped canned mushrooms, or mushrooms that have been sautéed in butter

MORNAY SAUCE *time: 14 to 22 minutes / yield: 3 cups*

to basic white sauce, add, before cooking, ½ cup grated Gruyère cheese and/or Parmesan cheese and an egg yolk lightly beaten

---

WINE SAUCE *time: 14 to 22 minutes / yield: 3 cups*

to basic thick white sauce, add, before cooking, 1 cup dry white or red wine

---

HOLLANDAISE SAUCE *time: 5 minutes / yield: 1½ cups*

4 egg yolks	put the egg yolks, lemon juice, and seasonings into the container of an electric blender and blend at low speed for 2 seconds
2 tablespoons lemon juice	
¼ teaspoon salt	
¼ teaspoon Tabasco sauce	gradually add the hot butter, and blend 2 seconds longer
1 cup hot butter	

in the absence of an electric blender, use a whisk and a little elbow grease, allowing about 15 minutes for the whole operation

161

RÉMOULADE SAUCE   *time: 5 minutes / yield: 1½ cups*

blend together 1 cup mayonnaise, 3 tablespoons chopped chives, 3 tablespoons chopped parsley, 1 teaspoon lemon juice, and a little Dijon mustard

TARTAR SAUCE   *time: 2 minutes / yield: 1½ cups*

blend together 1 cup mayonnaise, 1 teaspoon each finely chopped shallots (or onion), sweet pickle, stuffed olives, and parsley

NEWBURG SAUCE   *time: 7 minutes / yield: 2½ cups*

2 tablespoons butter	melt the butter, stir in the flour, mustard, and seasonings, and cook for 2 minutes
2 tablespoons flour	
pinch dry mustard	
few grains cayenne	stir in the cream, then the eggs, and finally the sherry
salt	
pepper	
2 cups light cream	
2 eggs, well beaten	
1 tablespoon sherry	

Haste doesn't make waste . . . it just saves time. So, cook it quick . . . but eat it slow. Enjoy!

INDEX

163

165